Working with British Rail

Hugh Jenkins

Batsford Academic and Educational Limited
London

For Michael, Christopher and Andrew

Typeset by Progress Filmsetting
79 Leonard Street, London EC2A 4QS
and printed in Great Britain by
The Pitman Press Ltd.,
Bath
for the publishers
Batsford Academic and Educational Limited
an imprint of B T Batsford Limited
4 Fitzhardinge Street, London W1H 0AH

British Library Cataloguing in Publication Data

Jenkins, Hugh
    Working with British Rail.
    1. Railroads—Great Britain—Vocational guidance
    I. Title
    385'.023'41   HE3015
    ISBN 0 7134 2684 5

Contents

Acknowledgment

I gratefully acknowledge the help I have had from a considerable number of people in the preparation of this book. As someone who has made a career in railway management, I know that many railway people over the years have influenced my perception of this great industry, and I hope if they read this book they will recognise their own unique contribution.

Particular thanks are due to many colleagues who have given me advice and information about the content of the book. Denzil Morgan was closely involved at the beginning of the project and helped me develop the structure and format of the book. I also received considerable help from my management colleagues on the London Midland Region and elsewhere, particularly David Maidment, Ian Brown, Ken Burrage, Douglas Power, Walter Marrian, Gerry Latham, Brian Burdsall, Terry Davies, Shelagh Avery, David McKeever, Jack Arling, Gordon Ford, John Baker, Steve Ollier, Bob Brown, Kevin Bramham, Malcolm Ramage, Ken Hardy, David Harrison, Eugene Heffernan and many others, particularly those who were kind enough to complete questionnaires giving details of a typical day's work. Extracts from these have been published. The mistakes, of course, are my own.

I am most grateful to Teresa Ward for her sterling work on the typescript and to Sally-Anne Houghton for some research support. A special word of thanks too to my wife, Barbara-Ann, who was generously tolerant of the personal inconvenience caused by so many of my weekends being taken up by this project.

Captions to illustrations between pages 44 and 45

Inside Crew Works, BREL
Construction of Inter-City 125 Power Cars

Modern electronic panel signalbox
Traditional mechanical lever-frame signalbox

Class 87 electric locomotive on Inter-City duties
Ticket collector at Station

Checking passenger tickets on train
Steward in Buffet Car Mark III catering vehicle

Shunter joining up electric multiple units
Diesel multiple unit maintenance

Booking Office at Milton Keynes Station
Cleaning the front end of an Inter-City 125

Train about to leave Paddington
Track relaying

Greasing points on the Permanent Way
Modern track maintenance machine in action

Reproduced by courtesy of British Rail

Preface

By *Sir Peter Parker, MVO, Chairman, British Railways Board*

We have heard so much about unemployment recently, that it is good to read a book about work, especially one about railway work. In recent years the Railway community, in common with much of British industry, has gone through a crisis of change. Nor is this process complete. In our search for productivity we have been reducing our staff numbers. We need improved productivity to unlock our potential, to work towards the bright future we all know to be within our grasp. In the future we will need less railway jobs than we have in the past. This has led to our imposing an unusually tight control over recruitment, so that natural wastage through retirements can take care of the manpower reductions. As a result many young people who tried to join British Rail in the last few years have been disappointed. There were not enough jobs to go around. But this cannot go on forever. And we need to find the railwaymen of the future.

This book gives us a timely reminder that Railways remain a major industrial force. There are still over 150,000 Railway jobs. We are still one of the biggest employers in the country and will remain so. Even though our workforce will reduce further as we move towards a better, more modern railway, we will remain a great national industry offering an extraordinary wide range of interesting and demanding work.

That is why we are determined to recruit and train as many young people as we can under present circumstances. There is a major task already begun, to modernise our system towards the goal of a popular, well loaded railway, competitive, giving value for money, putting the customer first and enjoying the esteem of the public. I promise you it will be fulfilling and demanding work—no less.

In this book Hugh Jenkins tells you about railways from the inside, how they work and what kind of work there is. I am confident it will help you discover if there is a railway career for you and if there is, that it will be rewarding and enjoyable.

London 1983

7

1 The World of Railways

Choosing a career is one of the most important decisions you will ever make in your life. If you make a sensible choice you will look back on it with pleasure and satisfaction, perhaps even for the rest of your working life. If you make a wrong decision you will certainly regret it and it could take you some time to recover, or as we might put it to 'get yourself back on the rails!'. That is why you should take extra care in thinking about your future career. Probably you do not have any direct experience to draw on, so you must try and discover as much as you can about the world of work. I suggest that what you really want is to find a job which will be both interesting and demanding, a job which suits the kind of person you are, one which gives you a chance to develop your skills and abilities. As you are reading this book you are obviously thinking about your career. Perhaps you are wondering what it would be like to work on the railways, and in this book I will try and tell you. It has been written to help you decide whether there is a railway career suitable for you. Even if you finally discover that railway work is not for you, that would still be worth knowing, so by reading these pages you would not have wasted your time.

In considering your future you don't want to rely on guesswork. You will want to make an informed choice. You will need to ask what kind of person you are, and what kind of work would interest you. You must discover what demands will be placed on you by the work you are considering. Will you be able to meet those demands? That is for you to decide. Railway work can be both interesting and varied, but like most other jobs there will be some necessary routine.

There is an amazing range of employment on the railways. You may feel that you are faced with a bewildering choice of careers, even if you rather like the idea of working for British Rail. In this book we will consider the full range of railway careers. As you would expect some railway jobs are specific to railways, but others are of the kind you would find in any large company. After all, British Rail is one of the largest businesses in the country, and it offers the usual range of commercial and industrial employment. For example, if you want to be a typist, an accountant, an engineer, a receptionist or a clerk, these are all jobs you could do with British Rail. As one of the largest employers in the country, British Rail offers almost every kind of work you could imagine. If you want to be an airline pilot, maybe you should look somewhere else. But if you want to pilot a cross-channel ferry between Dover and Calais, then talk to Sealink, our Shipping Company. And if you want to be a computer programmer, a waiter, a secretary, a rat-catcher, a chauffeur or a telephonist then come and talk to us. If you want to work with computers and video word processors we have some of the biggest systems in the country. And, of course, I almost forgot, if you want to be a train driver, well that might be possible too!

Nevertheless, it is important for you to appreciate that there is a lot more to railway work than driving trains. By the time you have read this book you will understand that; but within these pages I will concentrate mainly on those jobs which are specific to railways, rather than those which can be found not only in British Rail but also in any other large company.

What kind of person is required?

Railways are a public service. Many railway workers have to meet the public in the course of their work. Anyone who is thinking about taking on a job which means public contact must like meeting people and helping them. Have you ever noticed on railway stations how passengers need re-assurance? Are they on the right platform? Will they get on the right train? What time is the next train to Bristol? There is no end to the questions which can be asked. If you are on the platform in a railway uniform you will be expected to know the answers, and be polite and informative.

When the railways have a bad day, the customers have a bad day too. Occasionally there is a locomotive failure or perhaps a member of staff does not turn up for work in a key job and no replacement is available. Whatever the reason, the trains are running late. This has a 'domino effect'. When one falls down it knocks down the whole row. Likewise when a train breaks down it blocks the track for the following trains. A train which is running late is likely to be taking up timetable paths planned for other trains, and they will run late too. Now think about the customers. One passenger is on his way to London to catch the boat train. If he is more than half an hour late he will miss it. And he must be in Paris this evening because he has arranged to meet someone there. He begins to wish he had gone by air, which he dislikes. Maybe next time he will. Another passenger is a Sales Executive. He has an important meeting with a customer at which he hopes to clinch a deal. If he gets there late and flustered it all could go wrong. These understandable frustrations will be made known to railway staff, who will have to cope with the complaints with tact and understanding. But this is always second best. The real task is to run the railway efficiently so that the trains operate as they are supposed to in the timetable. This is the only result in which railway operators can take real pride, and a lot of effort every day goes into trying to achieve it.

The railways run for 24 hours a day. Many jobs involve shift work, and if you are not prepared to work irregular hours, this would disqualify you from many railway jobs. People quickly get used to shift work. While irregular and unsocial hours can be a disadvantage, many people find that shift work gives them more freedom to organise their lives to do the things they want to do, compared with a steady 0900 to 1700 type of job.

Railways are a very disciplined activity. It takes discipline to run trains at all. Trains are not like cars with complete 'freedom of the road'. You are only allowed to have one train at a time in any section of line. A train needs about a mile to come to a stop from 100 mph. This would be highly dangerous without the strict control of the signalling systems to guarantee this 'stopping distance' at all times. Train movements are carefully planned and expressed in the form of the timetable. It is the job of many railwaymen to see that this timetable works in practice from day to day. This needs care and attention to detail, and an ability both to accept responsibility and to work under supervision. You must be prepared to do what you are told. If you are easy going and like to please yourself whether you do what you are told or not, you will never be a good railwayman. This is especially true of safety rules, which are there for a purpose. If you ignore them lives could be at stake.

The transport industry

British Rail is such a huge and complex organisation that we may sometimes forget that it is an important part of an even bigger sector of our national economy, concerned with transport and distribution. Transport is the movement of people and goods from one place to another. It obviously has a vital and important role to play in modern society. Like many of the activities which are central to our lives, we take transport very much for granted.

Think for a moment what life would be like without transport. Most people would not be able to get to work. There would be nothing to buy in the shops simply because nothing could get to the shops. Raw materials would never reach the factories. Nobody would go away on holiday. Petrol would not be delivered to garages. Even if it were, that would not help much because in abolishing transport remember that we have got rid of cars and lorries too! Our big cities would grind to a halt. We would all have to go back to living in small villages and grow our own vegetables. It would put the clock back to the Middle Ages. But the feudal system could only support a small population. Without food imports many people would starve. And sitting at home awaiting our fate, we could not even watch television. No coal would be getting to the power stations and the electricity would go off, just as if we had forgotten to put a coin in the meter. It hardly bears thinking about.

The point being made here, of course, is to emphasise that anyone working in transport is helping to provide an essential basic service, without which no modern society could function at all. It is obvious from this that there will always be a demand for transport, and those working in the industry have the satisfaction of knowing that they are helping to provide an important and worthwhile service to the community. Transport contributes to the economic prosperity of the country by making everyone else's contribution possible. It holds everything together by keeping the elements apart. It provides vital links between home and work, ports and factories, producers and consumers. The main business of the transport operator is not to manufacture anything, but to provide a service by which to meet his customer's needs.

Within the transport industry there are organisations of various sizes. They range from the man who owns his own taxi or lorry up to some of the largest transport organisations in the country. British Rail is the largest transport organisation in Great Britain and one of the biggest employers in the country.

The railways as a public corporation

British Rail is one of the great national industries. In our 'mixed economy' some industries are privately owned and others, like British Rail, 'belong to the country'. This means that BR has been taken into public ownership. It is not run as a Government Department but as an independent Corporation. It has been given responsibility for managing its own affairs within a framework determined by the Government. Any Government is bound to conclude that a railway system will be needed to supply important national transport needs for the foreseeable future. If you join British Rail you can, therefore, be absolutely certain that you are joining a company with long term prospects although in the future, as in the past, the industry will have to change and adjust to maintain progress.

The railway network, linking all major centres

One of the differences between British Rail and other transport operators is that British Rail has its own private route network. A road haulier takes his lorry on the public roads, but BR owns the track as well as the trains. Look at the simplified map of the railway network. You will see that it covers most of the country. Certainly it provides important trunk routes between all the major centres of industry and population. There is almost certainly a railway activity within reach of your home. As you get to know the railway network and its traffic patterns you will learn a great deal about the economic geography of Great Britain. The principal Inter-City routes radiate from London; from Euston to the West Midlands, Manchester, Liverpool and Scotland; from King's Cross to Yorkshire, Newcastle and Scotland; from St Pancras to the East Midlands; from Liverpool Street to Cambridge and East Anglia; from Paddington to South Wales and the West Country; from Waterloo, Charing Cross and Victoria to Southern England.

The organisation of railways

The organisation structure of British Rail is complex. It is a very large organisation, and to make it manageable it is divided up in various ways. These organisation units reflect different levels of command, the geographical spread, the different functions and the separate businesses, all of which together make up British Rail.

The BRB and the Regions

At the top is the British Railways Board and its headquarters in London. This is where future policy is decided and where the overall management of the railway system is co-ordinated. The railways are so large that they are divided into Regions. These are the Eastern Region, the Western Region, the London Midland Region, the Southern Region and the Scottish Region. Each Region is a big railway system in its own right and is again

13

Simplified map of railway network

MAIN RAILWAY PASSENGER ROUTES

Inter-City services ▬▬▬▬

Other services
(for Scotland and Wales) ▬▬▬▬

0 20 40 60 80 100 MILES
0 20 40 60 80100 120 KILOMETRES

sub-divided into further management units such as Engineering Divisions and Traffic Areas. Each Region is managed by a General Manager and his team of senior managers.

The geographical organisation of railways is important because the industry is dispersed and management control over the railway system has to be exercised reasonably close to where activities are taking place.

The Sectors

There is also a need to manage the railways as a series of separate businesses and this is where Sector Management comes in. There are five sectors of the railway business. They are as follows:

The Inter-City Sector

This is a major commercial business providing fast, frequent, long distance passenger trains between major towns and cities. It links the major industrial and business centres of the United Kingdom in a network of services over the key railway routes. Sometimes it is mistakenly regarded as a monopoly. But the only monopoly it has is a monopoly of steel wheels on steel track. The reality is that of competition. The rail Inter-City services compete with private cars, coaches and aeroplanes. It has to be marketed aggressively. Within the sector are important market segments, passengers with different journey purposes. For example business, leisure, holiday, family and social travel are really quite separate markets which all make use of Inter-City trains.

The London and the South East Sector

Although commuting takes place around many conurbations, the sheer scale of the operation around London and the South East part of England has led to this being treated as a separate business sector. The sector is characterised by heavy peak flows in the morning and evening 'rush hours'.

The Provincial Sector

This includes the branch line, local and stopping services which feed the main network. It includes cross-country and trunk routes which are not considered to be Inter-City and also the deep rural branch lines, in Wales and Scotland for example. This sector also includes suburban commuter services in major cities outside London. Since this sector is unprofitable its continued existence depends on the recognition that it is part of the 'social railway' funded in part by central or local Government.

The world of railways

The Freight Sector

Freight is an important railway business, particularly concerned with the movement of raw materials and heavy industrial consignments. Significant elements include the 'merry-go-round' trains for bulk movement of coal between collieries and the Central Electricity Generating Board power stations, trainloads of stone, oil, clay, chemicals and motor cars. 'Speedlink' is a fast overnight service for general merchandise in modern wagons between main industrial centres. Many major companies have private sidings connected with the railway network. Freightliners Limited provide a nationwide service for container traffic with international links to the European mainland and Ireland.

The Parcels Sector

There is a parcels business too, and this specialises in urgent traffic going as 'Red Star' or 'Night Star' as well as providing major contracts for the Post Office and newspaper traffic. 'Red Star' and 'Night Star' are simply brand names for special parcels services operating between main centres.

The Regions

Although sector management determines policy and sets the cost and service targets for each of the businesses, the vast majority of railway staff are employed by one of the railway Regions. From the point of view of individual employees they would see themselves working for a particular Region. Even today Regional loyalties run deep, and many railwaymen will claim that their Region is the best!

In the Regional Headquarters offices and below the work is organised into departments. The main departments cover operating, passenger marketing, freight marketing, finance, personnel, planning, signal and telecommunications engineering, mechanical and electrical engineering and civil engineering. If you join British Rail you will most likely be attached to one of these departments. It might help, therefore, to give you a very brief introduction to the work they do.

Operating

If you are interested in the running of the railway you will find the operating side of railways quite fascinating. The railway operators plan the timetables and run the trains. It is their job to provide the services. Drivers, guards, signalmen and shunters are all operating staff. Operating is the railway equivalent of the production

16

function in manufacturing industry. Not only does it include running the train services, but also the work at stations, freight depots and marshalling yards.

Marketing (Passenger and Freight)

The railways are a business enterprise. Like other industries they need to plan their services in such a way as to meet the requirements of their customers. The passenger and freight marketing managers produce the 'commercial' specifications on which the train services are planned.

There is an interesting distinction here between the passenger and freight businesses. Every member of the public is a potential railway passenger, so the marketing and selling of the passenger business is not unlike selling soap flakes or chocolate. For example, you will sometimes see advertisements on television, aimed at a mass audience and encouraging rail travel. The freight business is different. The 'purchasing power' is concentrated into comparatively few hands—the transport managers of the very big industrial companies. In selling to them the railways rely more on direct personal contact face-to-face. There is no point advertising freight services on television. Why talk to 10 million people, when there are only about 200 really important buyers? It would be a waste of money.

The passenger is buying the product 'off the peg'. The train service has not been specifically designed around his personal needs, but on a statistical analysis of the patterns of demand from the public at large. In the case of the large freight customer though, he can get a 'bespoke' service custom-made to his specification. The freight marketing managers take pains to find out exactly what he wants and can tailor the service to his needs providing the cost-revenue sums come out right.

Finance, Personnel and Planning

Most big companies have specialist staff for these departments. The Finance Department on British Rail prepares the accountancy records of the business and provides information to help managers make proper business decisions. The Personnel Department deals with the people who work for British Rail. This involves the recruitment, training and development of staff, the payment of wages and industrial relations. The Planning Department spends its time thinking about the railway of tomorrow, and the investment that will be needed to bring it about.

Signal and Telecommunications Engineering

Without a comprehensive signalling system British Rail could not operate at all. In recent years modern signalboxes have replaced the old 'mechanical lever' boxes on many main lines. This complex modern equipment needs careful design and maintenance and this is where the skills of the S&T Department come in, although the older equipment also has to be kept in perfect working order for as long as it is needed.

Mechanical and Electrical Engineering

The Mechanical and Electrical Engineering Department of British Rail has the important task of designing the locomotives, wagons, coaches and trains and maintaining them in good repair.

Civil Engineering

British Rail has a very big Civil Engineering Department to design and maintain the track, tunnels, bridges, embankments, cuttings and structures.

A group of businesses

Although the railway business is by far the largest of the activities conducted by the British Railways Board, there are other sizeable businesses within the group.

British Rail Engineering Limited

BREL is a separate subsidiary company. It has large workshops and manufactures locomotives, coaches and wagons not only for British Rail but also for export to other countries.

One of the issues concerning the subsidiary businesses is whether they should return to private ownership. In 1983 the British Transport Hotels chain was sold to private buyers and other companies could also pass into private ownership.

Sealink UK Limited

Sealink is a shipping company and port operator within the group. It has 58 ships and operates 11 ports. It provides passenger, car ferry and freight services between the UK and Europe to the Channel Islands and the Isle of Man and across the Irish Sea. It operates services out of ports such as Dover, Folkestone, Fishguard, Holyhead, Heysham, Harwich, Portsmouth and Weymouth.

Freightliners Limited

Freightliners Ltd is a specialist freight company in the group. It provides industry with a transport service for large containers (often 30 or 40 feet long and 8 x 8½ feet) through its network of terminals. This is a good example of transport 'integration'. The trunk services between terminals are provided by special container-carrying trains called Freightliners, while the collection and delivery is done by road vehicles.

Travellers-Fare

As mentioned before, until quite recently the British Railways Board owned a large chain of hotels which were managed as a subsidiary business by British Transport Hotels Limited. But now only the train and station catering activity remains in BR control. This is known as Travellers-Fare. It is still a very large catering operation and is an important element in the range of services offered to passengers and other station users. Travellers-Fare is a business in itself. It is the catering wing of BR.

British Transport Police

There is a special police force which handles police matters on railway premises and on trains. It ranks alongside other constabularies and offers a wide range of police employment.

Competition

As I have already explained it is a mistaken view that British Rail is a monopoly. This you will quickly see when you consider what alternatives are open to the customer. Over most of the range of services and facilities it offers, British Rail is in a highly competitive position. Think of yourself as a business man. You are based in an office in central London and quite often you have to visit one of your firm's factories in Manchester. How are you going to get there? Clearly you have quite a choice. Firstly you could drive up to Manchester by car using the M1 and M6 motorways. Another idea would be to get over to Heathrow Airport and catch a plane. Finally you could go to Euston Station and take one of the fast Inter-City trains to Manchester. The attractiveness of using the train will depend on a number of factors including relative cost. If the service is fast, clean, punctual, frequent and reliable you are more likely to use it. That is why railwaymen must always 'keep on their toes' to ensure that railway services are more attractive than the alternatives.

Co-ordination

But it would be wrong for you to think that the different 'modes' of transport (rail, road, air, sea) are always in direct competition with each other. It makes sense for each mode to try and concentrate on what it does best. Many journeys involve more than one mode, and the pattern is one of sensible co-operation rather than outright competition. For example, the railways encourage people to use their cars by providing car parks at the stations. Most of the daily travellers ('the commuters') who come into London by train begin their journeys by car or bus. The family car performs a 'feeder' role and the railways perform a 'trunk' role. Each is doing what it is best suited to do. The two methods of linking the car and train for this journey to work are sometimes called 'park-and-ride' and 'kiss-and-ride'. Park-and-ride is where the driver leaves his car all day in the station car park. This is rather a waste of a good vehicle, so many families prefer 'kiss-and-ride'. The wife gives her husband a lift to the station. After kissing him goodbye she can keep the family car for herself during the rest of the day, until she meets him again at the station in the evening. These are examples of the kind of things you will need to think about as a railway worker. If you are to understand railways you have to understand the role they play in people's lives, why people travel and what they think about their journeys.

2 The growth of modern railways

Early beginnings

When we look at the modern railway of today it is sometimes difficult to remember that railways were invented over 150 years ago. This was long before cars, lorries, buses or motorways. The first railways came into existence in the era of canals and stage coaches. In fact it was the combination of railway transport and urbanisation (the growth of towns and cities) that made the Industrial Revolution possible. In the crucible of modern industrial society the railways were a vital element. They were in at the start. Most inventions of that time have long since disappeared. For example, have you ever seen a 'spinning jenny'? The reason that the railways are still with us today is that the basic concept was so powerful. It proved capable of supporting layer after layer of technical improvement. The basic concept is simple: Put steel wheels on steel rails. Haul bulk loads along guided tracks. You have a railway.

The early railways developed from colliery practice. It was in the mines that men first started to use horses to pull tubs of coal along crude tracks. The Surrey Iron Railway, which opened in 1803, provided a horse-drawn goods service between Wandsworth and Croydon. The first railway to be operated by mechanical power was the Stockton and Darlington railway in 1825. George Stephenson's early steam locomotive 'Locomotion' was used to haul both passengers and freight on this line. In 1829 his most famous engine, the 'Rocket', won the Rainhill locomotive trials. This was followed in 1830 by the opening of the Liverpool and Manchester Railway. This was a triumph for its Engineer, the same George Stephenson, who became one of the most famous of the early railway pioneers. His son, Robert Stephenson, went on to become equally famous as a railway engineer. His statue stands outside Euston Station in London. To get some flavour of the early pioneering days, we can look briefly at the career of another famous railway engineer, I K Brunel, of Great Western fame.

Isambard Kingdom Brunel

Few men have contributed more to Civil Engineering than Isambard Kingdom Brunel. His wide-ranging achievements included the Thames Tunnel, the Great Western Railway and the 'Great Eastern' steamship. He designed the famous Clifton Suspension Bridge over the Avon gorge in Bristol and the equally well known Royal Albert Bridge at Saltash near Plymouth. This took his beloved Great Western Railway over the River Tamar into Cornwall. The rugged Cornish landscape posed engineering problems but could not prevent the railway thrust to the West. Born in 1806, Brunel died in 1859 at the comparatively young age of 53, worn out from dedication and overwork. He died soon after his steamship, The Great Eastern, suffered an explosion passing Dungeness Light. He was not aboard at the time, but his spirits must have sank when the news came in. Brunel's life was a mixture of triumph and disappointment. He was a daring engineer, an innovator, a man of courage.

Ideas to build a line between London and Bristol were first voiced in 1825 and 1832, but the first approach to Parliament in the form of a 'Great Western Railway Bill' came in 1834. The proposal was to link London and Bristol, starting at both ends and later meeting in the middle. It was difficult to choose a route. Vested interests were involved. For example Eton College objected to dirty railways coming anywhere near them. The Bill was defeated. But a second Bill was presented and became law in 1835. Work began. Brunel's plans to bridge the Thames at Maidenhead resulted in a famous engineering triumph. He designed a bridge to cross the river in two spans. Each span was a flat arch about 40 yards long. His critics said the bridge would collapse under the weight of the trains. It did not. In 1838 the supports were removed and the bridge remained intact. Not for the first time in his life, and certainly not for the last, Brunel had proved his critics wrong.

Another exciting engineering feat was his building of Box Tunnel, through Box Hill between Chippenham and Bath on the Great Western Railway. Brunel's plan was for a tunnel nearly three miles long with a gradient of one in a hundred. His critics called it 'dangerous and impracticable'. In those days tunnelling techniques were primitive, needing thousands of navvies working in difficult conditions. Every week a ton of gunpowder and a ton of candles were used under Box Hill. Four thousand men and three hundred horses toiled for two years. At least a hundred men died in various accidents. How seldom do we pause to reflect on their fate, as we pass effortlessly through the tunnel today in our Inter-City 125 trains! When the tunnel was complete it was perfectly straight. On the 21 June, the longest day of the year, it is said to be possible to stand at the West end of the tunnel and see the sun rising through the Eastern portal. Perhaps Brunel was an astronomer as well as an Engineer.

At least twice Brunel was defeated. But on both occasions he was ahead of his times and it could be argued he was actually right in his ideas. The first was the Broad Gauge. The second was the Atmospheric Railway.

The Broad Gauge

When the first railways were built the distance between the rails was arbitrarily fixed at 4 feet 8½ inches. Some of the first coal wagons had been built to this gauge. What was good enough for coal was surely good enough for passengers. Or was it? Brunel the innovator liked to challenge accepted ideas. When everyone else was building these narrow gauge railways he conceived his 'Royal Road to the West'. It would be larger than life, just like he was. He chose a gauge of 7 feet. This would allow improved power, speed and stability in his trains. Perhaps he believed the other railways would be forced to follow suit. They did not. The narrow gauge was too well established elsewhere in the country. The argument became one of standardisation and not technical merit.

Brunel lost the battle of the gauges in 1846 when the narrow gauge was adopted as standard. And yet, had the railways been built to his ideas, there is no doubt that the scope for technical development would have been considerable, and many modern design problems eased. We would have had a better railway today if only his ideas had been adopted.

The Atmospheric Railway

The second example is Brunel's so-called 'Atmospheric Railway'. He built this in South Devon. It was a novel idea though not entirely original. Brunel, as an engineer of genius, was attracted to innovation. The idea of an atmospheric railway was to do away with locomotives and have trains pushed along by air pressure. Between the rails there was a hollow tube. Along this tube ran a piston to which the trains were joined through a slot with a leather flap. When air was pumped along the tube the train moved. Brunel

23

built pumping stations every five miles or so to provide the power.

He wanted to escape from the limitations imposed by steam locomotives. Every steam engine is a mobile power source. Brunel wanted to separate power and traction. In a sense he was anticipating the electrification of railways. On electrified railways power is generated at power stations and brought to the locomotive along the wires. The locomotive is not designed to make the power, just to use it. This is economical. Once again Brunel's ideas were ahead of his time, but he was defeated by the limitations of the mechanical technology of the day. The system did not work well and had to be abandoned.

Railway engineering

The railway system is full of engineering interest. Many famous stations, bridges and tunnels are still in existence today and very much taken for granted. In their day they were widely seen as daring and imaginative engineering projects. There is probably a fine piece of railway engineering within reach of your home. A good example of such a project is the Severn Tunnel. In 1872 the G.W.R. was granted an Act to build a tunnel beneath the tidal waters of the River Severn. It was a daunting engineering task with frequent floodings. The work was not complete until 1886. The tunnel is on the line from London to South Wales. It is nearly 4½ miles long and still needs continual pumping to keep it from flooding. Today you can travel smoothly from London to Cardiff scarcely noticing you have passed through it.

The age of expansion

In the great age of railway expansion many people believed that there was a fortune to be made by building railways. Hundreds of small companies were formed, often duplicating each others' routes, and competing against each other for traffic. It was sometimes a race to see who could first complete their line to a particular town. At its peak this building boom became so much of a risky gamble it has since been called 'railway mania'. The peak was in 1846 when no fewer than 272 Acts were placed before Parliament seeking permission to construct new railways. It seemed that the way to make a million was to build a railway. The same people today would probably be signing up pop stars and starting record companies. Not surprisingly, many of these early pioneers did not make the money they expected. Some finished up bankrupt with nothing left but their dreams. It was not until the 1920s when road transport developments first had their impact that the railways met real competition from other modes of transport. However, they were certainly competing with each other because the different companies were all operating independently, often over parallel routes. One legacy of this is the present railway route structure with its lines radiating out from London. Even today some towns and cities have more than one railway station whose origins can be traced back to the old company days.

The 1923 grouping

It was soon recognised that this wasteful competition would have to end. In 1921 Parliament passed the Railways Act which required the separate railway companies to amalgamate into groups. Four groups were set up in 1923:

The London Midland and Scottish Railway (LMSR)
The Great Western Railway (GWR)
The London and North Eastern Railway (LNER)
The Southern Railway (SR)

Each of these railways built its own locomotives and rolling stock. Under their control, the development of steam locomotives reached a new peak.

In 1935 the LNER 'Silver Jubilee' streamlined express achieved 112 mph on trial and went into public service between London and Newcastle. In 1937 the LMSR responded with their 'Coronation Scot' from Euston to Glasgow. In July 1938 the LNER steam locomotive 'Mallard' achieved a world speed record of 126 mph. The other railways also produced their famous steam locomotives. The SR produced its 'Battle of Britain' Class Pacifics. The GWR developed some of the most beautiful looking steam engines ever, with its famous 'Castle' and 'King' class locomotives. This full flowering of steam is seen by many as the age of romanticism in railways. The passing of the iron horse is still a matter of regret to a generation of nostalgic railway lovers who grew up in that era.

The LMSR, LNER, SR AND GWR continued from 1923 until 1948. Between 1939 and 1945 Great Britain and her allies were at war with Hitler's Nazi Germany and her allies. During this period the railways were run down badly. There was little new investment. It was a period of austerity when all available money was diverted to sustain the costly war effort. Many industrial parts of the country suffered bomb damage and since railways were always seen as good targets by enemy bombers, much damage was incurred to the railway system.

British Railways

After the war, there was a General Election which resulted in a Labour Government coming to power in 1945. It was the policy of the Labour Government at that time to take into public ownership what they called 'the commanding heights of the economy'. But given the railways' desperate post-war condition, 'commanding depths' might have been a better description! However the result was nationalisation and the appearance for the first time of 'British Railways'. The new BR was split into six Regions, later to become five.

In 1948 when British Railways was formed it had 20,000 route miles (52,000 track miles), over 6,000 passenger stations, 20,000 steam engines and 650,000 staff. It resembled an army, and they turned to a General to run it.

Railway modernisation

In 1955 a new 'Modernisation Plan' was published. It promised a new deal for the run-down railway system and a new generation of railway equipment. Steam would be abolished and replaced by electric or diesel traction. Track and signalling would be improved and investment provided in stations and freight facilities. In the late 1950s and early 1960s the railways received major investments and much of the 'Modernisation Plan' was implemented. This was very welcome at the time and a new generation of locomotives and diesel multiple units entered service together in large numbers.

But now, 25 years later, this is seen as a problem, because all of this equipment also became old together. Trains are no different from cars in one respect. Maintenance costs rise with age. The diesel and electric locomotive fleet is getting older and less reliable, needing increased maintenance attention. Many locomotives have now reached the end of their working life and have been scrapped. The diesel multiple units are now nearly all life-expired. It will take another large slice of investment to replace them and this has prompted fresh debate about the role of the railway system, its financial prospects, and the level of investment justified for the future. These are among the issues raised in the Serpell Report of 1983. Since one of the questions posed concerns possible changes in the size of the railway network, people compared this latest report to the famous Beeching Report published 20 years earlier in 1963, which eventually led to the closing of many of the railway branch lines in the 1960s.

The other side of the coin was the work done by the British Railways Board to modernise its trunk network. The Inter-City passenger services in particular had their standards of speed and comfort enhanced through electrification of the West Coast Main Line from Euston to Birmingham, Manchester and Liverpool. This was hailed as a major achievement at the time. Electrification was later extended to Glasgow. This was followed later by the introduction of Inter-City 125 trains on the main routes from King's Cross to Leeds, York and Edinburgh and from Paddington to South Wales, Bristol and the West of England. High speed trains are now also operating on the principal cross-country routes between the North East and the South West and on the Midland Main line between St. Pancras and Sheffield. This development enhanced passenger comfort and reduced journey times.

Railways and society

Railways have had an important influence on the social structure of the United Kingdom. They helped to create towns and cities by making possible the separation of home and work, production and consumption. Transport provides the link between factory and shop, house and office, raw materials and industry.

Because the facilities that people want (place of work, recreation, home, entertainment, friends, the pub etc.) are geographically separated it is only by some form of mobility that people can integrate their lives into a whole. The mobility which they are permitted within society determines their range of choice and the resultant quality of their lives. The London suburbs owe their very existence to the development of public transport, especially the railways.

Railway accidents

The development of safe railways is an interesting historical study. Every time there is a railway accident an inspecting officer is asked to investigate and make recommendations. This system has allowed railways to learn from their mistakes. Over the years the lessons learned from accidents have been used to influence railway law, modify working practices and improve the rules and regulations governing railway operating.

27

The modern railway

In this chapter so far we have looked briefly at the long and distinguished history of the railway industry. As Great Britain developed, so its railway developed in step and in tune. Railways have always been part of modern society and still have an important role in the movement of passengers and freight. Although parts of the system are clearly in need of further investment, there is plenty of evidence concerning what a modern railway can do. If railways are to survive as a major industry into the twenty-first century they will have to change and adapt in the future, as they have in the past.

The key elements of the modern railway are now known. They include safe, fast Inter-City services giving speed, comfort and quality at an acceptable price. The Inter-City 125 trains have set new standards here. They will be followed by a new generation of electric locomotives, by an electric version of the 125 for electrified routes and by the delayed and controversial APT (Advanced Passenger Train). This has an ability to corner at higher speeds through its tilting mechanism. When it has been proved technically and drive-end power cars built for the production trains the APT will be introduced at 125 mph initially.

Compared to other countries British Rail has a low proportion of its network electrified and there are likely to be major extensions of the electrified routes at some time in the future. Increasing use will be made of computer technology. Railways are a disciplined transport system and lend themselves to computer applications, hence the concept of the 'cybernetic railway'. Railway layouts will be drastically simplified in future, to avoid excessive maintenance costs and the planners will ensure that good use is made of all equipment. Manpower practices will change and more productivity obtained through one-man operation of trains and more modern working practices. New forms of technology such as radio signalling and lightweight, cheap railbuses will be used on rural lines. The freight services will be trainloads for bulk flows or Speedlink trains of specialist air-braked wagons between main centres of population. Freight-liners will provide container services for suitable flows, especially those passing through ports. The Channel Tunnel will open new marketing possibilities in European traffic, both passenger and freight. The big cities will remain dependent upon the railways for their principal commuter flows. But only a cost-effective railway providing value for money is likely to gain the long term political support needed to sustain the 'public service obligation grant'—which is how the Government gives revenue support to railways.

Most railwaymen know that this means change. Change is uncomfortable, but necessary. Railway managers know the potential of their railway system. At its best it can beat the opposition hands down. One coal train is obviously cheaper to run than 75 lorries. But the total costs of the railway system are high and there is plenty of scope for improving efficiency and doing more to help the customer. Some people fear change. That is understandable. But the railwayman of the future will be expected to accept the changes which are necessary. It is not just a question of new hardware. A modern railway needs a modern workforce. And that means new ideas and some departure from old traditions.

3 The elements of the railway system

Although the railway system is an enormous and complex network, it can easily be broken down into elements. Most railway staff feel that they 'work on the railways' in a general sense, but they can also identify themselves more closely with a particualar workplace — their own department, location and activity. For them their place of work is not really 'British Rail' but one of the many stations, works, depots or offices which together make up the system.

There are advantages in working for a large company. It is more likely to have proper systems of training and a wide range of promotion opportunities. Against this you may wonder if you are going to be 'small cog in a big wheel'. Will people really take a personal interest in you and your progress if you are one of over 200,000 working in the railway family? The answer is yes. And this is because you will be working for a local manager or supervisor. It will be part of his job to see that you do your work properly, and you will probably see yourself as part of his small workforce. It is possible to work happily in a small team within a very big organisation without feeling lost. In this way you get the benefits of working for a very big industry without being swamped by its sheer size.

Because the railways are a large public service industry most people get some idea about railway work just by travelling by train and observing the industry at work. Factories are more 'secret' in that their work goes on behind closed doors, and you would need to arrange a special visit or see a film in order to understand the kind of work that goes on inside.

Let us use a rail journey, then, to identify some of the principal elements in the railway system. Each element is an important part of the whole and has its special role to play within the total system. Each element creates its own pattern of work too, and the kind of railway work we are talking about will depend very much on which element we are considering. For example the kinds of work which you will find at a main line London Terminus are different from those you will find in a small country station, a carriage and wagon maintenance depot or on the trains.

30

Come with me now on one of the most exciting journeys in the world. Let us join an Inter-City 125 High Speed Train for a memorable journey from London to Edinburgh. As we journey North over this historic route, we will keep our eyes open and see what we can find out about the railways and railway work. This will be a voyage of discovery. By the time we reach Edinburgh we will have travelled nearly 400 miles in 4½ hours and we will have identified most of the important elements of the railway system. Each of these elements creates its own pattern of jobs as has been said, and this can lead us into thinking about the many different kinds of work which are done on the modern railway.

London is a fascinating city with lots to see, but anyone interested in railways will certainly want to find time to look at the famous railway stations in the capital. In the past, before British Rail was created, there were separate railway companies serving the main routes from London. One legacy of this is that instead of having one giant central station serving all of London we have a number of important stations which were once the London termini of famous railway companies. For example Paddington Station serves the former Great Western Railway (GWR) route to South Wales and the West of England; Euston Station serves the former London Midland and Scottish Railway (LMSR) route to the north west and Glasgow and finally Waterloo Station serves the former Southern Railway (SR) route to the south of England and the Dorset coast.

Today we are going to perhaps the most famous station of them all—King's Cross. This is a station steeped in history. It was built in 1852 and covers 15 acres of land. Ever since it was built the name of King's Cross has stood for speed. The ability of rail travel to combine speed and safety for main line passengers has always been the secret of its success. But there was once a time when speed was so highly prized at King's Cross that risks were deliberately taken. That was in 1895 and 1896 when the rival routes to the North decided to make a race of it, with the most powerful steam locomotives of the day. Some drivers even ignored the speed restrictions on curves to get there first. But before long the railway companies saw the folly of this and called a truce.

As we enter the busy station the first thing to do is find our platform and look at the train. The train that awaits us gleaming on the platform is an Inter-City 125, the holder of the world speed record for diesel traction at 143 mph. These trains have been allocated to some principal Inter-City routes including the East Coast Main Line out of King's Cross. The train has Mark III coaches between two power cars. Each power car contains a Ruston Paxman Valenta 12 cylinder diesel engine of 2250 horsepower designed to run at 1500 rpm. Each power car has four electric traction motors mounted on its bogies. The train is of comparatively lightweight construction to give it a high power-to-weight ratio. It has excellent braking characteristics—being designed to stop in the same distance from its cruising speed of 125 mph as conventional locomotive-hauled trains from 100 mph. This was an important design requirement, otherwise the entire signalling system would have had to be modified. High standards of comfort are provided on the train with comfortable seats, air-conditioning, wall-to-wall carpeting and smooth running, even at the sustained high speeds which these trains are required to produce day after day. But before we get too engrossed in the hardware, we should pause and take in the first of the elements of the railway system which we hope to discover on our journey.

Inter-City stations and main line termini

King's Cross station is an example of a major Inter-City station. As a terminus it is the end-of-the-line for people arriving in London. It is one of about 200 business and holiday centres which are served by the Inter-City network. The Inter-City route network is about 6,000 miles and every week day over 1,000 Inter-City and other express trains run over some part of this network. Over 8,000 million passenger miles are logged up on Inter-City trains every year. Clearly many railway jobs are located at passenger stations. There is a passenger station in nearly every large city in the country and so the opportunity to work at a station is available almost anywhere in the country. In a later chapter we will be looking at some of the jobs which can be done on stations, but it might be interesting to identify some of the main activities of the station. Firstly there is platform work.

Platform work

Platform staff help to load and unload parcels, to keep the station clean and tidy and assist passengers with their luggage. They must ensure that the doors of the train are closed before departure and that the train is ready to leave on time. They must also help passengers with their problems and give information and advice about travel. At junction stations where passengers change trains they may need to be directed to their proper train. You have to be polite to passengers. They are your customers and the money they spend on their tickets helps to pay your wages if you are a railwayman.

Platform work brings you into contact with the trains and passengers. It is an outdoor job, but mostly working under cover. On many large stations it involves shift work with the emphasis being on passenger trains in the day time and parcels trains or sleeping car trains at night.

Ticket staff

The next group of staff are ticket staff. It is the job of the ticket staff to check that passengers are entitled to travel and to advise passengers about train services. Sometimes they work at the ticket barrier, sometimes on the train. Sometimes they catch people without tickets when they collect the money that is owing to the railway. In cases of fraud, the passenger trying to cheat the railway of its revenue can end up in court and get a hefty fine.

Supervisors

There are various grades of staff working at stations, so that more senior, more responsible work will entitle the man or woman concerned to higher rates of pay. The station is controlled day-to-day by supervisors who make decisions in the interest of the efficient working of the station. For example they allocate staff to different duties, check the quality of the work done, do their best to ensure that trains run to time and try to think up better ideas for efficient work. They also hold back trains to wait for passengers connecting from a late running train if that is the best thing to do in the circumstances, and generally take charge of the work of the moment, coping with both normal work and sudden emergencies. Anyone joining the railways has the chance to become a supervisor after he has gained experience and seniority always providing he is good enough. The supervisors report to the Area Manager and his management team. Most Area Managers have a team of managers covering the principal activities. Typically there will be an Area Operations Manager, an Area Train Crew Manager, an Area Terminals Manager and an Area Administration Manager. Where an Area Manager covers a large geographical area, he will also have Traffic Managers at important locations and Station Managers at Inter-City stations. If you work at a station on the traffic side of the railway, one of these managers will be your ultimate 'boss' although it will be the supervisor who will be your immediate boss for everyday work.

Booking offices

Another important activity, particularly at large stations, is the selling job that takes place in booking offices. To work in a large booking office you have to be a clerical officer. This requires some educational qualifications or successfully passing the entrance examination for clerical officers. At the booking office windows the public buy tickets, so the people who work in the booking office must know the different kinds of ticket which are on sale and the rules which govern their use. For example you cannot sell a cheap day return for someone to use on a busy peak hour train. In the booking office tickets are issued and money taken. Since it is, like many railway jobs, a customer-contact job it would not suit anyone who is not prepared to develop the social skills of dealing with the public. On occasions this demands tact and diplomacy as well as the ability to explain things clearly. When we say 'the customer is always right' we really mean that he should be treated courteously, because we value his custom. But some customers can be very difficult to deal with and this can demand both patience and skill. Apart from being face-to-face with the customer, the booking office staff have to operate ticket issuing machines. Increasingly these are sophisticated electronic devices which provide analytical and accountancy data. The money itself has to be counted carefully and handled in a disciplined way, rather as if you were working in a bank.

Enquiry Offices

The whole basis of the railway service is the timetable. On some busy lines, the service frequency is so high that passengers need not bother too much about the timetable. At peak times on busy lines into London there may be a train every ten minutes or so, in which case passengers just turn up at the station rather like they would on the London Underground. But on the main Inter-City routes the service frequency is probably one an hour and passengers may need to check what time their particular train is due to leave.

They will do this by making a train enquiry, either on the telephone or by calling in person. Passengers who are particularly likely to want to use this facility are those who do not travel to their destination regularly. If they did they would probably know the train times already. Passengers who are making more complicated journeys involving connections, or where alternative routes are available are likely to need information. If the enquiry about a train service is made on the telephone it is likely to be handled at one of the Central Telephone Enquiry Bureaux. These can be found at many large stations, but you won't see them on your journey, because they are 'behind the scenes'. Typically they will be large rooms containing up to a dozen desks. At each desk sits a timetable expert. He or she must know the timetable frontwards, backwards and inside-out, and give information about services and fares to the person making the enquiry. If the enquiry is made in person similar information will be given face-to-face at the Enquiry Office or Travel Centre.

Travel Centres

At important stations the Enquiry Office role is carried out at one of the new Travel Centres. A Travel Centre is a shop window for dealing face-to-face with the whole range of a customer's travel needs, from train enquiries to seat reservations, holiday bookings, European rail travel and many other requirements. Those who work in travel centres have to be smart in appearance and become expert in the wide range of travel options and special promotions involved in marketing the modern passenger railway. They may have to deal with group bookings and business trips. Some travel centres can issue airline tickets.

The Area Manager's Office

Another activity behind the scenes is the management and administration of the station or area. In the back rooms are those who help to plan the work of the station, concern themselves with its budgeted costs and revenues and carry out the essential clerical and administrative routines to keep the whole place ticking over.

The Parcels Office

Another category of station work is the parcels office. Many companies send their urgent parcels by express train, particularly where the premium quality 'Red Star' service operates. Consignments of parcels are received in the parcels office, booked up and then taken to the platforms for loading onto nominated trains.

One thing you will have noticed is that it is not only railwaymen who work at stations. There are Post Office staff to load the mail onto the trains. Many of the big stations are little villages almost, with their own shopping and ancillary services. King's Cross has a branch of W. H. Smith, the newsagents which is bigger than that to be found in many towns. All around the station are bars and cafeterias.

Travellers-Fare

The catering facilities are provided by Travellers-Fare. The range of catering provision can be very wide, from small kiosks to refreshment rooms and restaurants. There is a French-type bistro restaurant at King's Cross. At other main line stations in London such as Waterloo, Charing Cross and Euston a MacDonald-style fast food hamburger operation is mounted under the trade name of Casey Jones, named after an American railroad hero. All of these outlets provide the usual range of catering jobs. So it means you can serve hamburgers and still work for British Rail.

'Right away driver'

I hope that you have not become so interested in what is going on at the station that you have forgotten we are going to make a journey. The big moment has now arrived and we must be off to re-join our train for the high speed journey to the North. At the precise time of departure, the guard consults his watch, gives a penetrating blast on his whistle and waves his green flag. This signal has been relayed to the cabin of the Inter-City 125. Smoothly the driver releases the airbrake and engages the enormous power of the diesel engines. With a characteristic shrill whine the '125' accelerates from the platform and begins the 400 mile journey to Edinburgh. We settle down next to one of the large picture windows and prepare to watch the passing scene. At the North end of King's Cross station is a large building which is a vital part of the railway operations in the area. Not many passengers give it a second glance. Very few realise what goes on inside. It is King's Cross Panel Box, part of the railway signalling system.

Railway signalling

There are two main types of activity concerned with railway signalling. Firstly there is the engineering side. The design, installation and maintenance of railway signalling systems is a very important task. Within railways, Signal and Telecommunications Engineering is a large department which provides employment opportunities throughout the country. Secondly, there is the operations side of signalling concerned with controlling the safe passage of trains along the track. British Rail is modernising its signalling system to replace older mechanical equipment by new electronic panel boxes. On this important route we have modern colour light signalling all the way as we have on most of the principal routes.

Traditional signalboxes are worked by levers and have mechanical interlocking frames. These manual boxes have to be close to each other because otherwise the sections between them would be inconveniently long. Only one train is allowed into a section at a time on any one track. The new power-operated panel boxes permit the remote control of many signals and points over a wide area. Some of the modern boxes cover 150 route miles. The operation is done by turning switches and pressing buttons to set up routes. The signals are multiple aspect colour lights, which have replaced the old semaphore signals on many lines. The King's Cross signalbox is an important control centre. As we travel North, the next panel box is as far away as Peterborough 76 miles away. In the King's Cross panel box, the signalmen observe the passage of the trains by coloured lights on a large diagram of the track layout.

Computer-controlled train describers ensure that as our Inter-City 125 moves from one signal to the next, the code number identifying it moves automatically to the correct new position on the diagram. The design, installation and maintenance of signalling equipment in the panel boxes and out on the ground by men from the Signal and Telecommunications Engineering Department is another vital aspect of railway work which the public rarely sees.

As soon as we leave King's Cross we pass over one of the most complex track layouts in the country. It is known as 'the throat'. King's Cross handles about 300 trains a day and they all converge on 'the throat'. The problem is there is so little room between the station and the first tunnel that great ingenuity has been needed to provide a layout flexible enough to cater for all of the train and locomotive movements. One of the advantages of the Inter-City 125 is that it can be driven from both ends. The train has a power car with a driving cab at each end. A locomotive-hauled train arriving at a dead-end terminus like King's Cross will trap the engine on the buffer stops. Another locomotive has to withdraw the coaches to release the train engine.

The 'throat' layout is so complicated that it would be impossible to reproduce it in a model railway without special designs. This famous layout is a reminder to us that many railwaymen work on the track itself, and that the design and maintenance of the permanent way is a very important part of railway work.

No sooner have we passed over 'the throat' than we plunge into the tunnel. There are two tunnels to the north of King's Cross, 'Gasworks Tunnel' and 'Copenhagen Tunnel'. With the power of the '125' behind us, we surge effortlessly up the rising gradient, hardly noticing that it is quite steep. Although the structure of the London buildings obscures any sense of the underlying geography, we are now climbing out of the Thames Valley.

Soon we will be passing close to Alexandra Palace which commands the higher ground to the left of the line. In the old days this climb out of King's Cross was not so easy. Steam locomotives were unable to draw heavy trains up through the tunnels and so it became normal practice to use 'bankers'. These are not men who lend money or even 'certain draws' to put on the football pool coupon! No, a 'banker' is what railwaymen used to call a second engine used to help push a heavy train up a bank. The second engine would run behind the train uncoupled. It used to push and shove as hard as it could until the train was up the gradient, when the driver of the banking engine would slow down and let the express pull away. With all the effort involved, the tunnels were rarely clear of smoke, which made them difficult and potentially dangerous places to work. In the walls of the tunnel are little cubby-holes into which maintenance staff can withdraw when trains are passing.

Locomotive and train maintenance

A few miles out of King's Cross and still gaining speed the Inter-City 125 passes the first of three important railway installations concerned with the maintenance of locomotives and trains. These depots employ many skilled maintenance workers. This is Finsbury Park Maintenance Depot at which diesel locomotives are maintained. Next we pass Hornsey Maintenance Depot where the suburban electric multiple units are maintained. Multiple units are diesel or electric trains which are made up from units, usually of two or three coach sets, each with its own power units. This type of train does not need a locomotive. Finally we reach the Maintenance Depot at Bounds Green. It is here that the

Inter-City 125's are maintained in running condition. Modern railway trains incur annual mileages which would frighten the average car driver. For example a '125' can log up a quarter of a million miles in a single year. The equipment must be strong, robust and well-maintained. It takes a great deal of knowledge and skill to keep the fleet in sound working order.

As we pass, we notice that groups of railway workers pause to watch us go by, just like many other members of the public. If you spend your time maintaining complex equipment there is a pride in seeing it in full working order. Some of those watching our train go past probably have been working on it themselves in the last few days. It is routine preventive maintenance which is the secret of reliability. No railwayman wants to see a train break down on the track, although it does occasionally happen.

The sight of the electric multiple unit sets at Hornsey reminds is that there is more to railways than Inter-City. In fact, as we pass some of these trains on the slower lines, we realise that the route is also a commuter route into London.

Commuter services

You will hear a lot about 'commuting' if you live near any of the big cities, especially London. The railway system has a number of important social roles, but none is more significant than the role of sustaining the big cities.

In the South East of England the whole social fabric and work patterns are based on daily mass passenger movements between places of work in Central London, the West End and the City, and where people live, in the suburbs or the country. Railway commuters are season ticket holders who travel to work by train each day. 'Inner Commuters' live in the suburbs within 15 miles or so of London. 'Outer Commuters' can spend over two hours a day just travelling to work. They live all over South East England, including places on the coast like Brighton. Often they are trying to combine the advantages of living in the country and working in London, where there are well-paid office jobs. Typical commuter stations on the route over which we are travelling are Welwyn, Stevenage and Hitchin. Two features of commuter travel are worth remembering. First, most people travel every day and buy season tickets. Second, there is a morning peak when everybody is off to work and an evening peak when they all arrive back home again. These are both very busy periods for railwaymen concerned with this type of traffic.

The elements of the railway system

Just as you are wondering if you would like to travel to London every day in the rush hour crowd our attention is drawn to a spectacular view. We are crossing the Welwyn Viaduct. The viaduct is 519 yards long. It was built in 1850 and its 40 arches carry our train 100 feet above the Mimram Valley. Suddenly we realise what a fine feat of civil engineering it was to build the railway system and we may wonder who maintains all of the viaducts, bridges, embankments and tunnels. In fact BR has a big Civil Engineering Department to look after these things in addition to maintaining the railway track itself. Soon afterwards our train slows down. The driver has read his Notices and has now seen the expected warning board at the lineside advising him that the track ahead is under repair. There is a system of advising drivers, through weekly booklets and Notice Board displays, of any temporary speed restrictions in force. He slows down to the required speed and the '125' coasts gently through the section concerned until he sees the board marking the end of the speed restriction.

Civil engineering

The design and maintenance of the railway track and of the bridges and tunnels is the job of the railway Civil Engineers. British Rail maintains all of its track, or 'permanent way' as it is usually called. It is interesting to realise that the maintenance of the track often has to take place while the train service is operating. That is easy enough for routine maintenance but for bigger jobs such as re-laying track and altering track layouts, there is a system which allows the engineering gangs to gain 'possession' of a track.

These possessions can be at weekends or in the middle of the night, when traffic is light or can be diverted. Sometimes the work has to be done in the limited period between trains. You can sometimes tell, as our driver has, where track maintenance work is being done, because special speed restrictions are imposed on all trains travelling over a line until the condition of track has been restored to normal. Drivers always keep a special look out for maintenance staff on the track and sound the horn to warn them of the approaching train. The track gangs are protected by a look-out man and are required to wear high visibility vests.

Track maintenance work is healthy outdoor work, but you would have to be out in all seasons and be fit and strong to do it properly. Sometimes passengers look out of the window and think,

'Look at all those men standing about down there doing nothing—that must be a cushy number!' What they do not realise is that the men have been working on the track over which the train is passing and have stepped to one side to let the train go through. As soon as the train has passed they will get down to work again and the look-out man will be keeping his eagle eye open for the next train. It is to help these men that the front end of trains are painted yellow, an easy colour to spot at a distance. Our '125' also has a spotlight on the front which can be seen a long way off.

As the journey settles down into a pleasant routine we hear a reminder over the train's public address system that there are buffet facilities on the train. It is time to investigate.

Train catering

There is a choice of catering on our train. As the businessmen settle down to lunch in the Restaurant Car, we decide to try the Buffet Bar '125'. Here there is a choice of hot snacks and various drinks. We decide to buy cokes and a couple of beefburgers, quickly cooked in the Microaire oven. The stewards are smart and cheerful. They run one of the fastest Buffet Bars in the world. Here is yet another aspect of railway work, train catering, where meals can be prepared and served up at 125 mph. As we leave the Buffet Bar some passengers are taking beers and spirits back to their seats. So we have a restaurant on wheels, a cafe on wheels and a pub on wheels! That's one way (or perhaps three ways) of catering for every taste.

By timing the train against the mileposts we work out that it is travelling at its maximum cruising speed of 125 mph. Almost before we realise it, we are approaching Doncaster. This is an important railway town and we look keenly out of the window in anticipation. Just South of the station we see the famous Doncaster Works of British Rail Engineering Limited.

British Rail Engineering Limited

Doncaster is one of the 13 main railway workshops. Some of the most famous steam engines in the world were built here. In particular the famous Gresley Pacifics (a Pacific is a steam loco with a 4-6-2 wheel layout; 4 for the leading bogie, 6 for the coupled driving wheels and 2 for the trailing axle beneath the cab). 'Flying Scotsman' and 'Silver Link' are names to remember. But the most famous of them all was the streamlined 'Mallard' which broke the world record for steam with its 126 mph in July, 1938, a record that will probably never be broken. Today Doncaster Works is producing the powerful Class 58 diesel locomotives for modern freight train working. At Doncaster can be found the full range of jobs you would expect to find in a major engineering works. BREL employ apprentices and skilled craftsmen in almost every trade.

Junction stations

Doncaster itself is an important railway junction and this is where the main lines to the Yorkshire industrial centres of Wakefield, Bradford and Leeds leave the East Coast route to Scotland. We are not going that way today, so we pull out of the station and head North for York.

York is a fine city, an important railway centre and another junction station where routes connect. The curved roof of the station is very elegant and it is well worth examining closely some of the detailed ironwork. York gives us the chance to note some more elements of the railway system.

Headquarters offices

The railway needs management and administrative offices. At York, a short distance from the station and inside the walls of the ancient city can be found the Headquarters Offices of the Eastern Region. The General Manager of the Region is based here and so are the Chief Officers of the Region. Reporting to this Head Office are Divisional Managers. On our route Divisional Offices can be found at King's Cross, Doncaster and Newcastle. British Rail's administrative structure is currently under review and is likely to be changed through the adoption of a two-tier management structure for the traffic organisation of the Regions eliminating the Divisional level. Clerical, administrative, technical and managerial staff not employed at stations and depots are likely to be attached to Divisional or Regional Headquarters. Interesting clerical work is available on all Regions in Headquarters Offices, where there are important departments covering the three main businesses— Passenger, Freight and Parcels—and also Operations, Planning, Finance, Personnel, Management Services, Civil Engineering, Mechanical and Electrical Engineering and Signal and Tele-communications Engineering.

Branch lines

York is also an important junction both for main line and branch
line services. The line from York to Harrogate is a typical branch
line. It has a diesel multiple unit passenger service and old-style
mechanical signalboxes. Branch lines serve local communities and
provide a feeder service into the main line. As we pull out of York
we press our faces to the window to get a glimpse of the National
Railway Museum. This houses a fine collection of railway
locomotives, including 'Mallard' and other historical relics.

The track between York and Darlington is straight and level,
ideal for high speed running. Soon we are coasting along at our full
125 mph. Another Inter-City 125 flashes past in the opposite
direction. At a closing speed of 250 mph, we scarcely have time to
register its passing before it has gone. This reminds us of an
important railway employee, the man at the front end of the train
on whose skill and experience we are relying for a safe journey.

Train crew

The operating staff who work on trains are called train crew. The
actual composition of the train crew will depend upon the type of
train and the particular circumstances. When most people think
about railway jobs it is probably the driver and the guard they
think of first, followed by the old-fashioned 'station master' and
'porter' although these no longer exist as job titles. Train crew are
a special kind of railway person. They actually work the trains and
need to be really expert in the safety regulations and signalling
practices which govern the movement of trains. The term train
crew includes drivers, assistant drivers, guards and conductor
guards. The manning arrangements will depend on the train we
are talking about. Under modern conditions such as those
applying on the electrified 'Midland Suburban' lines between St.
Pancras (London) and Bedford, one-man-operation of trains
applies and the driver does not need an assistant driver or a guard.

A brief stop at Darlington and once again we are off, this time to
Newcastle, another important railway centre. The Tyne crossing is
interesting. We cross the river on the King Edward railway bridge
opened in 1906. To the East we can see the new bridge carrying
the Tyne-Wear Metro system and Robert Stephenson's two-tier
high level bridge. Near Newcastle we notice a marshalling yard,
Tyne Yard.

The elements of the railway system

Marshalling yards

A marshalling yard is a group of railway sidings where freight trains are shunted and re-formed. Until recently Tyne Yard was a 'hump yard' where wagons could be sorted by gravity. At one time such yards were important in the network of yards dealing with miscellaneous wagon load traffic. Shunting locomotives would push rafts of wagons over the hump and points would be operated by power or manually to guide wagons into their proper sidings. In this way freight trains were formed. The development of modern freight services has reduced the network marshalling requirement, but Tyne is still an important yard serving local destinations around Tyneside and linking the North East into the national freight system.

Freightliner terminals

Now we are on the move again on the last leg of our journey to Edinburgh. Near Edinburgh is the Portobello Freightliner Terminal. The Freightliner system is a network of container trains working between terminals. At these terminals large cranes tranship the containers between the flat wagons of the Freightliner trains and the fleet of road vehicles which provide the door to door service. This is an important part of the railway freight system. The terminal employs staff to man the terminal itself and lorry drivers to collect and deliver containers at industrial premises. Some large works have private sidings so that freight wagons can be shunted in direct.

Our train is pulling into Edinburgh Waverley Station. It has been a really enjoyable and memorable journey and we look forward to our return trip. What have we discovered on this journey? Perhaps that there is more to railway work than we first thought, that people work in a great variety of locations and workplaces and that different parts of the system have different roles to play. Within each location we could find a range of jobs each contributing to the success of that role. Teamwork is clearly vital if the whole system is to work successfully. We will be looking at some of the individual jobs in later chapters.

Captions to photographs see page 6

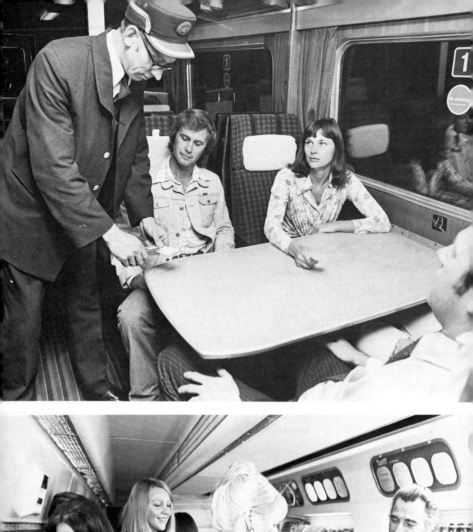

4 Railway work

It has already been mentioned that railways employment is very varied. There are so many different kinds of work to be found in British Rail, that it would be possible to write a book about each of them. Did you know, for example, that there is a Railway Medical Service? Before anyone is taken on they will be examined by a railway doctor. Afterwards they may be seen by a railway doctor at various stages in their working life. However, I doubt if many medical students are reading this book to find out if there are any career opportunities for them! If you want to find out what it would be like to be an architect, surveyor, salesman, clerk, accountant or secretary you should first read about those careers in general and then afterwards remember that there are jobs in British Rail for all these people. As one of the very biggest organisations in the country it makes sense that we should employ our own specialists in many fields. Most of these posts are not specific to railways. You can find them in many industries. This book does not attempt to provide a general guide to employment for those jobs which are found in any industry. If you think about it you will recognise that the requirements of the jobs are no different from one company to another. If you are likely to make a good typist working for the Midland Bank, then you are likely to do equally well in British Rail.

This book will, therefore, be more concerned to describe those jobs which are specific to railways. These are the ones you are most likely to be thinking about if you have picked up this book. And these are the ones which most people would first think about when they hear someone is 'working on the railways'.

British Rail is a huge concern but even so it is only part of a major sector of the national economy known as the transport industry. The transport industry is a very large industry which offers a wide range of employment. Administrators, planners, computer men, personnel specialists, marketing experts and many other corporate roles can be found as much in transport as in other types of organisation. But since British Rail is a labour-intensive industry and its locations widely distributed, the typical employee is involved in the operating activity, engaged in the physical movement of people or things.

Railway work

In this chapter will be described some of the general characteristics of basic railway work—the kind of jobs you will find on trains, on stations or in depots. These are the jobs directly concerned with the running of the railway, in the sense of traffic operations, and with the day-to-day maintenance of railway equipment—the locomotives, coaches, diesel multiple units, railway track and signalling equipment. We will look closely at individual jobs in later chapters. Here we want to introduce some general themes which will help you understand some of the characteristics of railway work. Like other forms of employment in transport, railway work does have special characteristics which set it aside from most other jobs.

The 24 hour railway

The railway system works around the clock. The main line passenger services over the Inter-City routes generally run between about 0700 and 2200. But at night the sleeping car services operate and the freight and parcels railway comes to life. If you went to a busy station like Crewe and spent 24 hours there you would see that it is a place which never sleeps.

As an example I would like to give you an indication of the level of activity at Crewe Station between 2200 and 0600, when you might mistakenly expect things to be somewhat on the quiet side.

You will find an extremely busy station with many railwaymen and Post Office workers on the night shift. During this period there are about 20 local train movements of electric or diesel multiple units. Some of these start or terminate at Crewe and have to be run empty between the station and the carriage sidings. There are no less than 33 Inter-City or provincial express trains calling at Crewe on the night shift. These include overnight trunk services and sleeping car trains. Many night trains carry substantial quantities of parcels, mail and newspapers. There are also about 25 trains dealt with at Crewe at night which are principally there to carry Post Office mail, Post Office parcels, railway parcels or newspaper traffic. This is an important sector of the railway industry where an overnight transit is required. Parcels vans have to be detached and attached to trains. Traffic has to be sorted and re-loaded. Locomotives have to be changed for movements to and from the non-electrified Chester and Holyhead route and train crew relief has to be provided. It all adds up to a hive of activity on Crewe Station at night. And what goes on at Crewe Station is typical of what you would find at many major stations.

You will see from this that Crewe Station is just as busy at night as it is in the day. A mile or so towards London from Crewe Station another railway installation is equally busy during the night hours —Basford Hall Yard. This is a focal point of freightliner and freight train movements, many of which take place at night. It is where freight trains change crew and sometimes change loco- motives. Freightliner trains arrive in sections and the trains are split and re-formed by the night staff, before speeding on through the night. On most main line routes the signalboxes which control the movement of trains must also be manned around the clock. Since trains are arriving and leaving at all times of the day and night, train crews are booking on and off duty at almost every hour of the day and night. The railway system never sleeps. The direct consequences of the 24 hour railway for ground level operating staff are, therefore, shiftwork and unsocial hours.

Shiftwork

For many kinds of railway work, particularly at stations and depots and in signalboxes, shiftwork is normal. To cover the full 24 hours, eight hour shifts are often worked 0600-1400, 1400-2200 and 2200-0600. If you are not prepared to work shifts, then railway operating work is not for you. Train crews are required to work irregular hours and to book on duty at times when work is available. This can mean very early shifts. If you book on at 0500 to take a train out at 0545 you may have to set the alarm clock for 0400 or even earlier. Railwaymen have to accept this as part of the job. This is a necessary feature of railway employment because the service of transport is in demand for 24 hours a day. Although there are obvious 'peaks' these tend to be early and late, and many employees are required to work shifts or irregular hours. This applies both to the conveyance of passengers and the carriage of goods. For example, to give the desired level of service to the customer, parcels and freight depots usually try to forward as much traffic as possible on the day the traffic is received. This involves the loading staff working well into the evening and night trunking to the destinations. The first train in the morning requires a driver and the last train home at night. Some railway staff book on at 0200.

This often means working in the evening or at week-ends when there is the greatest opportunity for social activity at the pub, watching television or other leisure pursuits. The requirements of shift work and unsocial hours impose certain constraints on the pattern of life of the individual affected. The arrangements within the family (meal times, bed times, family-centred social activities etc) have to be organised in such a way as to accommodate these demands. The employee may find himself inconvenienced by his conditions of employment. He will have to forego certain activities which he would want to pursue. He might regularly miss his favourite television programme. He may find leisure-time on his hands when his mates are at work and the pubs are shut.

These factors are naturally recognised in some form of shift-payment. In general the shift worker finds that his job makes greater demands on the way in which he organises his life, compared with the day worker, and it is clear that transport as an industry is prone to generate a great deal of shift working. Also the relative disadvantage of having to work week-ends has increased with the general adoption of the five day week in manufacturing industry, because not only is the railway a 24 hour industry, it is a seven days a week activity. You may have to work on Saturdays with a rest day in the week. Sunday work is normally overtime except where special work patterns have been agreed.

Security of employment

Railway jobs offer relatively secure employment and recruits coming into the industry, particularly in times of economic uncertainty, may be consciously opting for a job that provides a regular steady income, which they can rely on. You could be made redundant in your job if it were no longer needed but the railway would always try and find other work for you if possible.

Variety of work

Most transport jobs have in-built variety and a reasonable level of interest. They provide opportunities for the job holder to work part of his time in the open air.

Transport as a service industry

Like hairdressing, poodle-clipping and window cleaning, railway transport is a service. This sets it apart from manufacturing industry which produces a physical product which you can put in a shop. If you are a manufacturer, you can produce a product and then sell it afterwards. This has two advantages. Firstly, your production line is not continually open to public inspection so your mistakes do not get noticed, unless you try and sell the defective product afterwards. Secondly, you can inspect your product for quality and withdraw defective items before sale. This quality control enables you to have confidence in the product which you put on the market.

The transport operator is in a very different position. His 'production line' is his service and it is under public scrutiny. Worse than that, production and consumption are taking place simultaneously. This may help economically (no money tied up in unsold finished goods or work-in-progress), but causes problems. If the poodle-clipper snips off the dog's tail by mistake he cannot go the store room for another. If the train breaks down, the customer is bound to suffer. The product is highly perishable and cannot be stored. An empty seat-mile is lost for ever.

The implications of this are far-reaching. The operator is extremely vulnerable. It is the *service* industry, strangely enough, which has the greatest difficulty in providing an acceptable level of service. And as a railway employee you are in the front-line. You are highly visible to the public. The railway's mistakes are seen. You are constantly dealing with members of the public using the service. These encounters tend to call on social skills which you need to develop. Because you are dealing with the public and providing a service, the employee has a public job to perform. When the service breaks down you are there to bear the brunt of the immediate criticism, whether it is actually your fault or not.

Geographical spread

Many transport undertakings have a wide geographical spread with employment locations scattered around the operational area. British Rail employs people in several hundred locations. This has the advantage that railway work may be found near where you live. The effects on an employee of belonging to an organisation with geographical spread are several. Your relationship to your organisation will be affected. The headquarters management may well seem very remote and you will tend to identify with the local unit. On the other hand you are likely to have friends and contacts in other parts of the system and may well have cause to visit other depots and stations etc in your work. Train crew, of course, are travelling around all of the time. For many this is one of the attractions of the job. If you are looking for promotion in a large dispersed organisation you are likely to have to move fairly often because job opportunities can crop up at another station miles away from where you work.

The geographical mobility of the job

Transport industries provide their operating staff with the opportunity to move around during the course of their working day. Although a train driver may be tied to the timetable more than a lorry driver (who usually has more freedom in terms of route-selection and work-placing) he would probably compare his lot favourably (in this respect) with a factory worker tied to his bench, who gets no change of scene. One of the attractions of traffic operations work is that in many jobs you will be 'out and about' and not tied to a desk or workbench. The advantage of this lies in the variety which it brings to the job. You may see more of the country than you would from other jobs. This is true in many jobs in transport. In the case of air travel, the romance of exotic places gives an aura of glamour to the job of the air hostess, which goes well beyond the objective content of the job, which is to act as waitress in a badly-designed restaurant! Not all transport jobs permit movement. Many staff are based permanently at stations, depots, signalboxes, offices or maintenance workshops but mobility is a very common feature.

Responsibility

All railway work carries some responsibility. If you are sorting and loading parcels you are expected to handle the traffic carefully and avoid breakage or damage. You must also load the parcels onto the right trains. Customers don't like their parcels ending up in Bristol when they wanted them to go to Cardiff!

But some railway jobs are responsible in a special kind of way. These are the jobs which carry special responsibility for the 'safety of the line' as railwaymen call it. The obvious examples are driver and signalman. These jobs demand a thorough knowledge of the complex rules and regulations governing train working and signalling practice, and a knowledge of how to respond in an emergency. Railways are a very safe method of transport because they work to a very disciplined set of rules.

The jobs require care, attention to detail and concentration. Above all the drivers and signalmen must know what they are doing and do it with skill and experience. Railwaymen are proud of their industry's safety record. It is a measure of their skill at running the railway properly.

Jobs in British Rail

To give you some idea of the range and scope of railway employment, you may be interested in an analysis of the numbers of railway staff by Region and grade group. This shows in the table below which is the actual position at the beginning of 1983.

Analysis of railway employment— British Railways staff numbers

Salaried

	A	B	C	D	E	F	TOTAL
Eastern	1706	4203	2679	847	262	59	9756
London Midland	1496	4779	2838	981	292	56	10442
Scottish	663	1841	1135	411	87	32	4169
Southern	1235	3008	1769	566	125	81	6784
Western	935	2196	1317	436	95	57	5036
BRB (Rail)	2535	2797	50	733		45	6160
BRB (Corporate)	889	597	18	259		1872	3635
TOTAL	9459	19421	9806	4233	861	2202	45982

KEY A = Managerial, B = Clerical, C = Supervisory, D = Technical, E = Traffic Control, F = Other

Wages

	G	H	I	J	K	L	M	N	TOTAL
Eastern	6891	3263	2291	5938	8117	373	5200		32173
London Midland	6603	3393	2106	6427	8978	305	5255	10	33077
Scottish	2710	1322	829	2486	3281	105	2097		12830
Southern	3796	2158	959	4987	4820	152	3984	19	20875
Western	3054	1532	816	2951	4172	142	3169	11	15847
BRB (Rail)					14	234	68	97	413
BRB (Corporate)					1	43	119		163
TOTAL	23054	11668	7001	22789	29383	1354	19992	137	115378

KEY G = Footplate, H = Guards etc., I = Signalmen, J = Traffic, K = Engineering, L = Miscellaneous, M = Workshop, N = Other

Total number of staff

Eastern	41929
London Midland	43519
Scottish	16999
Southern	27659
Western	20883
BRB (Rail)	6573
BRB (Corporate)	3798
TOTAL	161360

Railway work

It is important to note that some of these jobs are in the 'entry grades' and others are 'promotion jobs'. You will progress into the promotion grades as a result of your suitability, seniority, qualifications and training in comparison with others who may be competing for the same posts. Within the industry there are recognised 'lines of promotion' through which members of staff can progress by steps. These are known as 'promotion diagrams'. Two examples of promotion diagrams are given below, covering wages grades in the Civil Engineers and Signal and Telecommunications Engineers Departments respectively:

Sample promotion diagrams

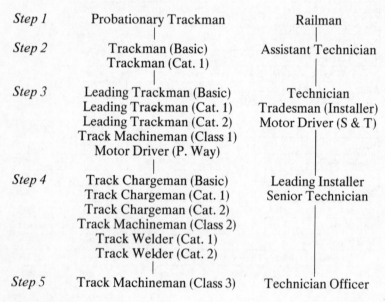

Step 1	Probationary Trackman	Railman
Step 2	Trackman (Basic) Trackman (Cat. 1)	Assistant Technician
Step 3	Leading Trackman (Basic) Leading Trackman (Cat. 1) Leading Trackman (Cat. 2) Track Machineman (Class 1) Motor Driver (P. Way)	Technician Tradesman (Installer) Motor Driver (S & T)
Step 4	Track Chargeman (Basic) Track Chargeman (Cat. 1) Track Chargeman (Cat. 2) Track Machineman (Class 2) Track Welder (Cat. 1) Track Welder (Cat. 2)	Leading Installer Senior Technician
Step 5	Track Machineman (Class 3)	Technician Officer

Railway industrial relations

The railway industry has strong Trade Unions and there is a formal system of industrial relations which is of long standing. There is an underlying procedural agreement between British Rail management and the railway Trade Unions which is one of the most comprehensive agreements of its kind in the country. It establishes the system of industrial relations to which both sides work. The system can handle both negotiating items and those where management is consulting with staff to seek their views on various proposals. It is a representative system under which discussions can take place at three principal levels:

1   At local level   (Local Departmental Committees)
2   At Regional level   (Sectional Councils)
3   At National level   (RSJC, RSNC and RSNT)

In general local issues will be discussed at local level. The staff representatives meet management in a committee. This is known as the LDC (Local Departmental Committee). In some circumstances, where the local committee cannot negotiate an agreement or when matters affecting more than one location are involved, an issue can be dealt with at Sectional Council. This is the next level in the 'machinery of negotiation' which is what railwaymen call their system of industrial relations committees.

At Regional level there are different Sectional Councils for the main groups of staff. Councils have both management and Trade Union membership. One Council covers salaried staff; another covers footplate staff; a third covers traffic staff and a fourth covers technical staff in the permanent way and signalling activities.

Because the railway system of industrial relations is highly centralised, the important discussions on pay and conditions of service take place nationally, through the Railway Staff Joint Councils (which are also organised into sections covering the main groups of staff) and the Railway Staff National Council which discusses major issues, such as the annual pay talks. One aspect of the railway system which is rather different from that in many other industries is that there is provision for an independent Tribunal to arbitrate on disputes which management and Unions cannot resolve for themselves. For example, in 1982 Lord McCarthy, the Chairman of this Tribunal, was asked to consider some productivity ideas linked with the pay deal. You may remember that there was a railway strike in early 1982 over 'flexible rostering' which was one of the productivity items under discussion.

When you join the railway you will be expected to become a member of one of the Trade Unions recognised by British Rail. The law on 'closed shops' is changing and the railway industry may have to reconsider its position, but at the moment all new entrants are required to join a Trade Union as part of the present membership agreement between railway management and the Trade Unions recognised by the British Railways Board. These are:

Railway work

1 *NUR*

The National Union of Railwaymen is an 'industrial union' representing all grades of railway staff with the exception of the Professional and Technical Salaried Staff employed in the Engineering Departments.

2 *ASLE & F*

The Associated Society of Locomotive Engineers and Firemen is a specialist 'craft union' representing the majority of drivers and others in the footplate line of promotion.

3 *TSSA*

The Transport Salaried Staff Association is a 'white collar' union representing clerical, salaried, professional and technical, supervisory and management staff in the railway industry.

4 *CSEU*

The Confederation of Shipbuilders and Engineering Unions represent the workshop craft grades in the railway workshops.

5 *BTOG*

The British Transport Officers Guild also has representative rights for senior managers.

From your point of view as a new recruit, much of the information above is really for background only. An important thing to remember is that you are entitled to direct access to your manager to explain any problems or air a grievance; also that there will be elected representatives who can represent you and your colleagues in formal discussions with local management. You will have certain rights and privileges, but you must also recognise your duties and responsibilities. In general, railway industrial relations is reasonably good, and this is especially true where there is trust and good will on both sides, in a spirit of co-operation to get the jobs done properly and iron out problems and difficulties.

Pay and conditions

Rates of pay and conditions of service are decided at National level. This provides an agreed rate for each job. In some cases there are opportunities to earn enhanced wages through attaining skills, meeting performance targets, undertaking additional work which qualifies for extra payment, or sometimes just by overtime or rest-day working when required. Railway work offers pensionable employment, and whatever your grade, there will be a modern pension scheme for you.

Travel concessions

One of the special benefits of working on British Rail is that after you have been working for six months you will become entitled to an allocation of free tickets each year, and qualify for 'privilege ticket' travel at about a quarter of the full fare. Many railway workers use this facility to travel around the country to visit friends or family, or just to visit parts of Great Britain they may not have actually seen. Have a look at the railway map in this book. How many of the places on the map have you been to? The chances are that there are many places you would like to visit. Another advantage is that you can get cheap travel to and from work. This is quite an expense for many people, but as a railwayman you will benefit by the cheap travel arrangements which are well worth having.

Training and education

Widespread facilities for staff training exist on British Rail. Some training takes place 'on the job' and some in Training Centres. It is British Rail policy to provide the training which will equip a member of staff to do his present job properly and prepare him for future responsibilities. Clearly many of the jobs on British Rail need substantial training support. For example a train driver needs a full knowledge of what he is required to do, how the signalling system works and a mastery of the many detailed rules and regulations covering the safe operating of trains. He needs to be trained in driving techniques in general, and in relation to the type of traction on which he will work. He also has to have a detailed knowledge of the routes over which he will work trains, and he needs to keep all of his knowledge up to date. But what is true of the driver is true of other grades too. You will be trained to the standard required of the job. You will also be encouraged to understand how your job fits in to other people's, to take pride in your work and see yourself as a member of a larger railway community whose role in life is to serve the transport needs of its customers, while at the same time providing an important element of the social fabric of the country.

British Rail as a non-discriminatory employer

British Rail is a non-discriminatory employer, committed to the recruitment and promotion of all grades of staff on the basis of merit and service, without regard to race, colour, creed, sex or marital status. Full consideration is given to the abilities of disabled persons.

Although there is no sex discrimination in British Rail, it is a matter of observation that most women employees are found in locations like offices and carriage cleaning where female workers have been well established. The hard core of operating and maintenance jobs are still something of a traditional male preserve. This is partly for historical reasons, but also because the work can involve both shiftwork and strenuous physical effort. In fact until recently few women actually considered employment in these areas. This is now changing and there is encouraging evidence that women can succeed in a number of these roles; as engineers, in locomotive cabs, in signalboxes, as supervisors and as managers. But we have a long way to go yet before we become a balanced work force, and women entering some parts of our business still need a little pioneering spirit although they need have no doubts about the welcome they will get.

5 Railway jobs — operations

In this chapter we will look at some railway jobs in the Operations department. These are the jobs which keep the railway running day-by-day. If you join the Operations side of British Rail there are two main streams of entry. You join either as a member of the wages staff or as a member of the salaried staff. As a member of the wages staff you would join as a 'railman' and your work would be outdoors. As a member of the salaried staff you would join as a 'clerical officer' and you would work indoors in an office. If you join as a school leaver under 18 years old you would be recruited as a junior railman or junior clerk, unless you came in as a trainee of some sort. In looking at Operations jobs, we find that they are grouped into jobs on stations, jobs on trains, shunting jobs, signalling jobs and Headquarters jobs. Let us takes these in order:

Jobs on stations

Jobs on stations are either wages grades ('blue collar') or salaried grades ('white collar').

Station wages staff

In an earlier chapter we had a look around King's Cross Station and saw the various activities which took place there. Now we want to look at particular grades and their duties. The railway wages grades are known as 'versatility grades' because each grade covers a wide range of duties. You will find the same grade structure in stations or yards, so you must not think that these posts are confined to station work. Furthermore, these grades are likely to be altered in a restructuring exercise, although the range of duties to be covered will remain the same.

Railmen
The basic adult wages grade job on a station is that of the railman. On a good, efficient station the railmen are on their toes because they have a wide range of jobs to do all concerned with keeping the flows of traffic moving and helping members of the public. We do not call any of our station staff 'porters' any more. The term

'railman' covers the old 'porter's' duties and lots more. But that does not stop some passengers calling for a 'porter' if they want some help with their baggage, although these days the self-help trolleys are mostly used for this purpose. Railmen are expected to perform a wide range of labouring duties, such as sweeping up, loading and unloading traffic, cleaning various equipment and tidying mess rooms. They may also be called upon to sort documents, answer telephones, check parcels and record the arrival and departure of trains. Their platform duties include attending trains, labelling luggage, marshalling trolleys, operating lifts or hoists and marking platform edges. In sheds or yards railmen operate carriage washing machines and perform various general duties.

One of the most important tasks of the platform staff is to ensure that, when the train is ready to depart, all the doors are correctly closed and the train leaves on time. Safety is paramount. Passengers have appointments to keep and connections to make so nothing must delay departure. If a door is seen to be open the train must be stopped at the next signal, or a passenger could fall out. Railmen working at a terminus may have the additional responsibility of preparing the train for its next departure by cleaning it and providing water and provisions for the next journey. New trains like the Inter-City 125 High Speed Train can have a 'turn-round' time of as little as thirty minutes so railmen have to work efficiently.

After the parcels office staff have ensured that parcels are properly packaged, labelled, charged and paid for, the parcels are taken by railmen to catch the nominated trains on the express 'Red Star' system or loaded into special British Rail trolleys to be sent later in the day. The Parcels Office may also deal with left luggage and lost property. You need a good knowledge of the train services and parcels routes to be a railman or clerk involved with parcels. Time is crucial. A whole factory may be halted waiting for a certain part to be sent across the country before it can resume production.

Other railmen's duties include clearing and tidying the platform or helping passengers with their luggage. All platform staff must be prepared to answer queries from passengers about train departure times, platform numbers, arrival times, refreshment facilities and anything else a passenger may wish to know. A railman, like a booking office clerk, must pay close attention to the needs of the customer. Other sources of information such as public address systems, passenger information systems and closed circuit television aid the railman in his task. The railman is the entry grade. If a railman wants promotion he can apply for higher graded posts at the station.

Leading railmen

The next grade up from railman on a station is leading railman. Once again this is a broadly-based grade that can cover a range of duties. The duties of leading railmen can be varied according to where they are employed and what needs to be done. Sometimes their duties involve paperwork, such as recording and issuing stores, dealing with routing correspondence, obtaining signatures, weighing, stamping and charging for parcels traffic, collecting cash and maintaining records.

Leading railmen on platform duties are expected to collect tickets and raise excess fares, announce the arrival and departure of trains, attend to indicators and destination boards, ensure the security of premises, deal with left luggage, detach and attach vehicles on trains and handle seat reservations. They can be employed to operate weighbridges, attend to lost property, sort, code and check parcels, prepare delivery sheets, perform shunting operations and numerous other duties of a similar nature. On a station the staff employed on ticket collection and examination are generally leading railmen. In some parts of the country British Rail is moving over to the idea of 'open stations'. This means that passengers can buy their tickets at the booking office and are then free to walk onto the station without having to go through a ticket barrier. Where this system has been adopted the passenger's ticket will be checked on the train. Another variation can be found on rural railways, for example, where the small stations and halts may not be staffed at all. In this case a 'pay train' system operates and the conductor guard on the train sells tickets rather like a bus conductor does.

At the ticket barriers leading railmen check that the passenger has a valid ticket. Protecting railway income is extremely important on British Rail so the leading railman ticket collector needs to know how to recognise a wide variety of tickets. He must also ensure that the passenger knows which train to catch and give advice about the running of train and which platform the train will go from. He must also know the charging system and be able to raise excess fares.

Leading railmen are found performing a range of duties in the parcels office. Parcels come in different shapes and sizes. When parcels are brought in they must be checked. Are they properly packed and labelled? Are they bulky and awkward? Do they contain dangerous goods, such as chemicals or explosives which can only be handled on special conditions? When a customer brings in a parcel he completes a document known as a 'consignment note'. This is the contract to carry. The parcels must then be weighed and charged, coded and sorted. Later they are taken from the parcels office to the platform in a caged trolley known as a BRUTE and then loaded onto a train. In the case of 'Red Star' parcels, the customer can choose which train his parcels go on. Special arrangements are needed to make sure the 'Red Star' parcels catch their particular train. Often there is somebody to meet the train at the other end. He is a customer too. If the parcel does not arrive there will be a row. And it will be your colleague at the other station who will get the 'ear-full' not you, even though it was your mistake. It happens the other way round too! Since railways are a national network, the teamwork must involve other stations as well as your own.

Another example of a leading railman's job would be a man working alone in charge of a typical small station. He would have to issue and collect tickets, take cash and balance his books daily and do all the jobs needing to be done at that station, keeping it tidy and secure, and looking after the passengers. Some stations will have a booking office clerk working a 0900 to 1700 turn, supported by two leading railmen, early and late, who issue tickets in the absence of the booking clerk.

Railmen and leading railmen are also employed on carriage cleaning duties. Often this work takes place at night because the coaches are worked in the day. At large depots modern washing plants, which look like a big car wash, look after the exterior cleaning.

Senior railmen

The next job up from leading railman is the senior railman. He is mostly found on large stations where staff work in teams. He is a leader of the men in the lower grades. He takes part in the work and accepts responsibility for the proper performance of the work of his group, and for keeping up quality standards. For example, there may be a team of men involved in an activity such as shunting. One of them would assume personal responsibility for the work of the others. He is the senior railman. Similarly a group of railmen on platform work may be allocated to a group of platforms and placed in the charge of a senior railman who is the leader of that team. Sometimes a man working alone can be graded senior railman if his responsibilities are particularly heavy. For example, if a man is placed in charge of a small station which has a heavy responsibility in terms of the number of passengers joining and alighting, the amount of revenue earned or the frequency of the train service, these factors could be recognised in a senior railman's grade—even though the individual is not leading a team.

Chargemen

Chargemen are appointed where it is necessary to co-ordinate the activities of groups of men, each of which may be led by a Senior Railman. A chargeman is expected to take part in the work of the grades for which he is responsible. He will ensure proper performance of work within his control and use his own initiative to solve local difficulties in the day-to-day work. He also implements decisions made by supervisors and managers above him. For example, where the work of platform staff and shunters needs to be co-ordinated, it is the chargeman who must keep his eye on both activities and take decisions in the best overall interest of station working.

Station catering

Although it is not strictly railway Operations, there are other openings for those who would like to work on the catering side of stations. Travellers-Fare operates a large range of station catering retail outlets. These include restaurants, cafeterias, tea-rooms, bars and kiosks. A new development is the 'Casey Jones' hamburger operation providing 'eat-in' or 'take-away' facilities. The catering jobs are broadly based as shown below:

Post	*Duties*
Catering Assistant *Senior Catering Assistant*	These are retail and catering members of Travellers Fare station staff. They perform a wide range of duties concerning the preparation and serving of food, making products available for display, serving the customer and cleaning the premises.
Supervisor *Senior Supervisor*	Supervisors assist with the other catering duties while taking responsibility for the stock, the quality

continued overleaf

61

Railway jobs—operations

Post	Duties
	of service and the staff employed in the outlet.
Crew member	Catering Assistants in Casey Jones outlets are known as crew members.

The kind of person who would do well here is someone who likes meeting people, has the ability to cope with the full range of duties and is prepared to 'muck in' with the clearing up necessary to keep a busy outlet clean and presentable.

There are supervisory and management posts within Travellers-Fare.

Station salaried staff

Clerical staff

At large stations there are a range of clerical posts to be found. These posts are graded from Clerical Officer 1 (C.O.1) which is the starting grade, up to Clerical Officer 5 (C.O.5) which is on the threshold of management. Posts are graded according to their responsibility. Clerical work at stations falls into two broad categories: those which are involved in customer contact and those which provide administrative support behind the scenes. Taking customer-contact jobs first, these are to be found in booking offices, enquiry offices or travel centres.

The difference between the three offices is in the service they can offer. At a travel centre in a large station, the passenger can book a complete holiday in Great Britain or on the Continent including reservations at hotels and travel insurance. An enquiry office will be able to answer any of the passengers' questions about the journey and can help them book a number of services such as Motorail. The booking office will sell tickets and answer questions directly related to the train services at that station.

To be a station clerk involved in a customer-contact role is to be British Rail's representative with the travelling public, selling rail transport. You will need to be able to read British Rail and Continental timetables, make up booking office accounts, issue passengers with tickets and seat reservations and give the correct change. It is surprising how many people find difficulty in understanding a railway timetable. This is probably because it only makes sense if you understand the underlying route structure, and how this is depicted in the timetable format. As an example we include an extract from the timetable covering the West Coast Main Line between Scotland and Euston:

Scotland and North West England to the Midlands and London

	①	①	A ✕ ☎	B ☎	C 50	50 ①	D ✕ ☎	E 50	50 ①	50	✕ ☎	D ☎	G 50
Inverness ... 230 d				23ᵃ50									
Aviemore ... 230 d				00 50									
Aberdeen ... 229, 241 d													
Dundee ... 229, 241 d				04 08									
Perth ... 229 d				05 48									
Stirling ... 229 d						06ᵖ50							06p50 06p50
Glasgow Central ... 222, 226 d	07 10			07 23		08 10							08 23 08 30
Motherwell ... 226 d	07ᵃ26			07ᵃ39									08ᵃ39
Edinburgh ... 47, 225, 228, 241 d				07 06									08 06
Haymarket ... 47, 225, 228, 241 d				07 09									08 09
Carstairs ... a				07 44/07 53									08 44 08 53
... d				07 58									08 58
Lockerbie ... d													
Kilmarnock ... 222 d													09 04
Kirkconnel ... d													
Dumfries ... d					08 42								10 08
Annan ... d					09 01								
Carlisle ... a	08 33			08 53		09 22/09 30			09 37				09 53
... d	08 35			08 55		09 32/09 50			09 54				09 56/10 13
Windermere ... d						09 49			09 49				
Oxenholme ... d						10 17			10 21				10 40
Barrow-in-Furness ... d						09 20			09 23				
Morecambe ... d						10 10			10 10				
Lancaster ... d	09 29			09 49		10 34			10 38				10 57
Preston ... a	09 51			10 01		10 56			11 00				11 20
Blackpool North ... a				10 42					11 39				
Bolton ...				10 57					11 50				11 55
Manchester Victoria ...				11 15					12 08				12 15
Sheffield ...													13 29
Derby ...													15 26
Nottingham ...													14 50
Blackpool North ... d	09 06			09 20		09 50			10 18				
Preston ... d	09 51			10 02	10 11	10 56			11 00/11 00				
Wigan North Western ... d				10 16					11 14/11 14				
Liverpool Lime Street ... a				11q18					12 08/12 08				12q37
Warrington Bank Quay ... d				10 29					11 27/11 27				
Liverpool Lime Street ... d	10 00			09 25					10 35/10 35/11 20		11 25		
Runcorn ... d	10 17			09 45					10 55/10 55/11 37		11 42		
Stafford ... 82 d				09 58					11 08/11 08				
Crewe ... 82 a				10 54	10 59				11 53/11 53/12 00		12 06		
Holyhead ... d				08 15					09z20				
Manchester Piccadilly ... d			10 15/09 45		10 34		11 15		09 45/10 45		11 36		
Stockport ... d			10z23/09 56		10z42		11z23		10 56/10 56		11z44		
Wilmslow ... d			10z31/10 07						11 07/11 07				
Crewe ... d				10 57	11 02	11z10		11z36	11 55/11 55	12 03		12 08	
Macclesfield ... d					10 56		11 37			11 13			
Stoke-on-Trent ... d					11 16		11 57			11 42	12 15		
Stafford ... d					11 38		12 00		12 17/12 17/12 27				
Wolverhampton ... a				11 40	11 56		12 21		12 44/12 50				
Birmingham New Street ... a				12 00	12 20		12 46		13 04/13 10				
Birmingham International ... a				12z27	12 47		12 58		13 32/13 22				
Coventry ... a				12z38	12 58		13 09		13 44/13 44				
...keley ... d													
...field Trent Valley ... d													
...sworth ... d													
...eworth ... d													
...erstone ... d													
...neaton ... d					11z57						12 52		
Leicester ... d											13 36		15 31
Rugby ... 66 a				11 51					12 54/12 54				
Northampton ... 66 a				12 34					13 34/13 34				
Milton Keynes Central ... 59, 66 a				12 16	12 31				13 54/13 54		13 26		
Bedford Junction ... 59, 66 a			12z26	12z38	12 59				14 34		14 34		
London Euston ... 59, 66 a	12 38	12 49	12 59	13 10	13 20		13 35		14 00/14 23	14 10	14 20		

All seats reservable on this train. For details, see pages 10 to 21. Passengers are strongly advised to reserve seats as accommodation may be limited

A   ✕ and ☎ Mondays to Fridays, ① Saturdays
B   ☎ Glasgow to Wolverhampton
C   5 June to 18 September. From Llandudno dep. 09 21 (Table 83)
D   ✕ and ☎ Mondays to Fridays, ☎ Saturdays
E   29 May to 25 September. From Llandudno dep. 09 30 (Table 83)
G   5 June to 28 August

c   Until 2 October
e   Liverpool Central (Table 100) Change at Preston
f   Sundays to Fridays
g   Saturdays arr. Birmingham International 12 27, Coventry 12 55

p   Via Glasgow Queen Street and Glasgow Central. Passengers make their own way from one station to the other. Inter station bus link available. For details see page 65

q   Liverpool Central (Table 100)

Railway jobs—operations

You will have to be able to communicate clearly with some passengers who rarely travel by train and those who are simply confused or awkward. Passengers will need your help. Upon your attitude and the way you do your job could depend whether that passenger travels by train next time. The job demands both knowledge about railway services and skill in dealing with members of the public.

The information available on travel, and the methods of issuing tickets and making reservations are changing rapidly with computerisation. You will work with more sophisticated systems as British Rail seeks to provide the customers with a better service. The qualities needed are that you should be alert and presentable, show enthusiasm, patience, tact, sympathy and cheerfulness.

Clerks are also employed in certain large parcels offices, for example on accountancy and customer liaison duties, and also to ensure that the parcels office runs efficiently. Behind the scenes at stations there are a number of other clerical jobs concerned with the various office procedures which are needed to ensure the smooth running of a station. For example, clerical officers are needed for keeping staff records, budgetting, operating computer terminals and general administration. All station clerical staff have the opportunity to compete for promotion to more senior posts in headquarters offices of the kind described later.

Supervisors and managers

Supervisors

The main responsibility for controlling and directing station work falls upon the supervisors and managers of the station concerned. Supervisors are salaried staff who are responsible either for particular activities or for everything going on within their patch. For example, a carriage cleaning supervisor would be solely responsible for making sure his carriage cleaners turned out coaches cleaned to the right standard, both inside and out. And a platform supervisor would have full responsibility for everything which happened on his group of platforms on his shift. There are five grades of supervisor (from 'A' up to 'E') which reflect the level of responsibility. This provides a line of promotion up the supervisory chain, and an opportunity to reach management posts.

Managers

Whether you join British Rail as a railman or a clerical officer you could, if you were good enough, progress to the job of the local Area Manager or become a member of his management team. The

Area Manager is in charge of the activities on the stations within his Area. If anything unusual occurs the Area Manager or his Assistants are there to resolve the difficulties. The Area Manager holds overall management responsibility for the efficient running of railway activities under his control. At major locations an Area Manager can have up to 2,000 staff under his command, including train crew based in his area and working around the system.

The Area Manager has a team of managers to help him in this task. A typical Area management team is shown below:

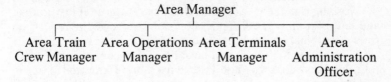

Area Manager

| Area Train Crew Manager | Area Operations Manager | Area Terminals Manager | Area Administration Officer |

Jobs on trains

The second group of jobs we will look at covers the work which takes place on the trains themselves. For many of you who are keen on railways, the idea of actually working on trains would have a special appeal. The jobs on trains which are covered on this section are grouped into train crew, Travellers-Fare train catering and travelling ticket inspectors.

Train crew
On the operating side of railways 'train crew' covers traction trainees, drivers' assistants, drivers and guards.

Traction trainees and Drivers' assistants
If you want to become a driver you need to begin as a traction trainee and be trained to become first a driver's assistant then a driver. This process takes a minimum of three years. You learn about the locomotives you will drive, the rules and regulations for safety on British Rail and the details of the routes over which you will work. When you are a qualified driver you may drive both freight and passenger trains of different types.

In some circumstances locomotives need to be 'double-manned' either by a driver and a driver's assistant, or in the case of the Inter-City 125 trains, by two drivers. There is an agreement between British Rail and the Trade Unions which covers this. It is called the 'single manning agreement'. Broadly it provides for locomotives and multiple units to be single-manned, except in

65

certain circumstances. For example at present locomotives have to be double-manned if they run at over 100 mph, if the turn of duty exceeds 350 miles, if there is steam heating equipment which needs attention or if there is more than 2½ hours continuous non-stop driving of an Inter-City passenger train.

Before anyone can be appointed to be a driver he must qualify as a Driver's Assistant and then pass an oral and practical examination. You will not become a driver until you have worked at least 500 turns as a driver's assistant and proved your competence in rules and regulations, and your understanding of the working timetable. You must demonstrate your ability to read and interpret all types of signals correctly, and to write reports on traction subjects. You must know the braking systems and the rules governing their use. You must be able to comply with freight train loads procedures. You must have a good knowledge of the various components which make up traction units and basic fault diagnosis. You must also pass a practical test in the interpretation of signals and judgement of distances, in the actual application of rules and regulations on the job, in driving technique, in the preparation and disposal of traction units and the ability to work with different types of freight train.

Drivers

For many young children there could only be one possible reply to the hoary old question, 'What do you want to be when you grow up?' and that is the classic answer, 'I want to be an engine driver!' It has always been a special kind of job and that is just as true today in the days of diesel and electric traction, as it ever was even in the heyday of steam locomotives. Driving is divided into two categories—train drivers and shunt drivers. Train drivers work passenger and freight trains over main lines and branches. Shunt drivers are confined to shed and yard working, within defined geographical limits.

Let us look at the job of the driver in more detail. It is the train driver who is responsible for the safety of the train throughout its journey. The driver must observe and act upon signals and speed restrictions. Before setting out on the route, the driver must familiarise himself with any temporary changes to speed limits or track layout. The driver must stop the train at the booked stations, giving the passengers as comfortable and punctual a journey as possible.

The knowledge and skill required of a driver is quite considerable. This knowledge falls into a number of categories:

Rules and Regulations For safety reasons, every possible aspect of train working and signalling is covered by detailed rules and regulations. These set out what needs to be done under both normal and emergency conditions. A train driver must be familiar with the Rule Book and particularly 'Section H' which covers the working of trains. In this section the duties of drivers and assistant drivers are listed. There are proper procedures for starting trains, for observing signals, for working in fog and for using the horn. For example, a driver must sound his horn as a warning when entering or leaving tunnels. There are rules for dealing with irregularities or obstruction, for stopping trains, for working freight trains with unbraked wagons and for stopping near 'catch points'. Catch points are spring-loaded points placed on a steep gradient to divert and derail any runaway train or vehicles away from further danger. Other regulations cover working two locomotives in tandem, going to assist another train which has failed, responding to equipment failure or emergency and many other aspects of his job.

The driver must know all of this. He must understand the meaning of all the signals and other lineside signs. He cannot usually ask anyone for help. He must rely on himself. The safety of 500 passengers may depend upon his knowledge, skill and judgement. There are regulations governing the speed at which he can drive and he must always anticipate, because it can take up to a mile to stop a train from speed. So unless the driver applies his brakes at the correct moment, he could overshoot a station.

Different types of train have different permitted maximum speeds depending on the class of traction and the formation of the train. He must, therefore, know the formation of his train and what it is permitted to do. He must also try and run his train in accordance with the Working Timetable. Unlike the public timetable this is a private timetable for railway staff. It shows all passenger and freight movements and gives passing times at key points so the driver can keep to time.

Traction knowledge Even if you are a skilled driver, you cannot just jump into any train and drive it away. Each locomotive or multiple unit has its different controls and driving characteristics. It feels different to be driving a Class 87 electric at 100 mph, than it does to drive a Class 56 freight locomotive at 40 mph with a 40 wagon coal train. Before a driver is allowed to drive a particular class of locomotive he is trained to drive it and

67

must be 'passed out' by a traction inspector.

Route knowledge A car driver can get into his car and drive anywhere, even if he has never been there before in his life. Not so a train driver. Before he is allowed to drive over a route he must be 'passed out' over that route. A record is kept at the train crew depot of every driver's 'route knowledge'. This is always kept up to date and drivers are given 'refresher' training if they need it to keep this knowledge current.

No driver is ever asked to drive over a route which he has not 'signed for'. The reason for this is obvious. The driver must know the route intimately. He must know the track layout, the permanent speed restrictions, where to expect the signals and the location of signalboxes and stations.

He must also know the gradients of the route and where to find emergency telephones. He must always know where he is on the line, and how to operate his train in those locations, like yards and private sidings which are covered by special instructions. He must know where to start slowing down and where to speed up, if he is to take advantage of the authorised line speeds and stop at the required stations and still keep on time. Each day the driver must read his weekly notice and special notices. These advise him of additional speed restrictions for engineering work. He must take these into account when driving his train over those sections.

He must be able to observe all of these matters in the hours of darkness and during fog. Most main lines are equipped with devices which provide an automatic warning audibly in the cab to back up the sight of the signals.

Link working Drivers are arranged into links. A link is a group of drivers who share the same jobs in rotation. Usually a variety of jobs will be covered by a driver over a cycle of about 12 weeks or more.

Guards

The guard is another member of the train crew. The guard is trained in safety and operating regulations and like the driver is required to learn the routes over which he will travel. The guard is responsible for the safety of the passengers and the train. At all times the guard carries a set of safety equipment including flags, a lamp and detonators to warn on-coming trains if the line gets blocked in an emergency. On a freight train the guard has to check the way the train has been made up, its weight, content, locomotive power, the effectiveness of the brakes and the safety of the load. Along the route the guard must be ready to apply the brake in an emergency or on a steep gradient. If the train is delayed at a signalbox he must find out why. The guard may also have to detach and attach wagons along the route.

The duties of guards are set out in detail in the Rule Book and the safety of the train may well depend on the guard knowing these rules and observing them scrupulously. There is no scope for carelessness. It is responsible work. Many aspects of the guard's duties arise from the operational and safety requirements of the job.

But in addition they have responsibilities towards passengers. They are expected to operate the public address system on the trains to keep passengers informed about the journey itself and train facilities provided. The guard must check that the train is in a clean condition, the toilets fully equipped, heating, lighting and other equipment in proper order and report deficiencies. In helping passengers, the guard is expected to have particular concern to look after the aged and disabled.

On Inter-City trains the guard may be required to inspect tickets and deal with passenger enquiries. On 'pay trains' which work along routes where there are unstaffed stations and halts, guards issue tickets on the train, collecting the money from the passengers to hand in to a main booking office later. Information must be given before departure advising passengers of calling points, catering arrangements and any expected delays. Stops must be announced on approaching stations and passengers advised to take all their belongings with them. During breakdown or emergency, or when the train is delayed the guard must keep the passengers informed about what is going on.

Where suitable conditions exist, modern passenger and freight trains are capable of running without a guard. This is happening already on the new Bedford-St Pancras electrified passenger service and the principle will be extended where appropriate. One of the ideas being developed is the 'trainman's concept'. The traditional line of promotion from steam days was engine cleaner, fireman, driver. Under modern conditions it makes sense to open up a line of promotion from guard to driver, but there have been practical difficulties in getting agreement to these changes which affect ASLE & F and NUR members.

Travelling Ticket Inspectors

One of the jobs which is done on trains is that of the Travelling Ticket Inspector. The TTI's are graded as supervisors and have a range of responsibilities. They work in teams and their two main functions are to promote passenger welfare and prevent fraudulent travel. They check tickets on trains and raise excess fares. If they detect serious fraud they produce the evidence that can lead to prosecution. Sometimes they work on trains individually or in pairs. At other times they may mount special anti-fraud campaigns giving blanket coverage to particular trains, stations or routes. They also provide a source of advice and help to passengers and assist in passenger control at major events such as football matches. They are not really operating staff. Their role is more commercial, concerned with the successful marketing of the product and the protection of revenue. However it is convenient for us to mention them while we are considering jobs on trains.

Train catering staff

Every day Travellers-Fare provides meal or refreshment services on about 850 trains, varying from a traditional restaurant car service to a buffet bar or even a simple trolley service. There are 380 vehicles in the catering fleet and over 1,600 staff are employed on train catering.

Some of the main Inter-City trains are executive trains, with full restaurant car and buffet services. These are facilities which enhance the attractiveness of rail travel to the businessmen using the service. Where there is full catering provision on an executive train there can be seven Travellers-Fare employees on board. These would be a Chief Steward, a cook, a steward/cook and four other stewards. The cooks prepare the food in the kitchen or buffet while the stewards serve it to the passengers. The chief steward is in charge of the catering activity on the train. Stewards wear smart red and blue uniforms and deal with the public, while the cooks work skilfully behind the scenes. Travellers-Fare recruit staff with experience of cooking and train them to become train cooks. Stewards need not have previous experience, but need to have the right kind of personal qualities for this type of work.

The scale of catering provision varies from train to train and route to route, reflecting customer demand. Where there is just a buffet car meals are not cooked and the buffet car is manned by one or two stewards.

Shunting jobs

The next group of jobs is concerned with shunting. Shunting is the attaching and detaching of wagons and coaches to and from trains.

70

Shunting can be done on passenger or freight trains to alter their formation. Shunting takes place in stations, depots, marshalling yards and sidings.

Passenger trains normally run in fixed formation sets. Nevertheless there are occasions when coaches have to be formed into trains at depots and vehicles taken out of formation for maintenance attention. At some stations parcels vans have to be detached or attached to passenger or parcels trains and sets of coaches worked empty between the station and the carriage sidings. All of this involves work for shunting locomotives and shunters.

Shunters are graded leading railmen and their task is to attach and detach these coaches and assist in controlling shunting movements, many of which have to be 'propelled'. Propelling is when an engine pushes a raft of coaches rather than pulls them.

The job of the leading railman shunter is very much an open air 'all weathers' type of job. It usually involes shiftwork, working around the clock. At many places the busiest period is at night, when freight and parcels trains are more in evidence.

A shunter at a passenger station must know what he is doing. He must get between coaches at the station and connect or release the screw couplings. He has to join up or disconnect the flexible hoses of the continuous air brake and vacuum brakes systems and see to the electrical connections. He needs to know the detailed regulations governing shunting movements and signal to the drivers of shunting engines in such a way as to control the safe movement of coaches and vans in attaching and detaching movements.

Another type of shunting takes place in freight marshalling yards and sidings where trains are divided up and re-formed and short local trips made into nearby depots and sidings. Freight trains involve more work for shunting staff. The movement of freight is recorded in a computer system known as TOPS (Total Operations Processing System). This is a 'real time' computer system with a very large main frame computer in London, with computer terminals on-line to it from every major location. The database is continually updated, so that a current record is available of the composition of every train, the contents of every siding and yard and the whereabouts of every wagon. The system is used for a whole range of management purposes beyond this. If a customer wants to know where his wagon of chemicals or trainload of cars is, British Rail can tell the customer immediately. Clerical officers operate the TOPS computer terminals at the Area

Freight Centres. The shunter receives various lists of wagons from the computer. He knows the composition of every train before it arrives. He knows the destination of every wagon so he can plan shunting operations. It is his responsibility to ensure that the trains are properly formed and ready to leave on time. He must be aware of the contents of the wagons and avoid any dangerous combinations of substances.

Once again freight shunting is a job which involves shiftwork and some exposure to the vagaries of the weather. You have to be quite tough and hardy to cope with a cold winter night in a typical marshalling yard. Trains have to be put into their right formation because they may have to drop off wagons at sidings and destination yards en route. The leading railmen shunters have shunting poles for uncoupling and coupling wagons. Modern freight rolling stock is air-braked and the coupling procedures are similar to that for passenger rolling stock. The days of loosely coupled, unbraked wagons are strictly numbered. Also with the change in the structure of the freight business, there is a sharp reduction in the requirement to marshall trains at intermediate points. Consequently under modern conditions the freight business needs fewer staff than it did in the past. Railfreight now specialises in complete trainloads of one product for a single destination, in company trains chartered by a single customer and in high speed wagon load traffic over trunk routes, marketed under the brand name 'Speedlink'.

Another factor which has led to less marshalling and shunting is the establishment of the Freightliner system. Freightliner depots provide crane power to tranship containers from road to rail or vice versa. In one sense this is a marshalling activity because it involves both sorting consignments and forming trains. The crane acts as a substitute for the shunter who would have done this job had the consignment been forwarded by conventional freight services.

Signalling jobs

Signalling is a very interesting and important activity on British Rail. It is the job of the signalmen to set routes for the movement of trains over complex track layouts and to work the signals which authorise the movement of trains. Signalmen must know all about signalling systems and methods. These are covered by detailed instructions contained in the Rule Book and Block Regulations. Signalmen are responsible for both the safety and punctuality of trains.

In an earlier chapter it was explained that there are two distinct types of signalbox in which signalmen can work; the traditional mechanical box and the modern panel box.

Since signalboxes vary from the quiet box on a sleepy branch line, to a busy main line London terminus, there is a system for classifying signalboxes and the men who work them into six grades from Grade 'A' at the smaller end right up to Grade 'F' at the top end. This classification is based on an assessment of the traffic workload of a signalbox and the scale and complexity of its equipment. It provides a promotion ladder from the smallest box to the biggest.

Working in mechanical signalboxes
Signalmen working in mechanical signalboxes are doing their job in the traditional old-fashioned way. During their shift they will normally be alone in their signalbox. All along the route will be a series of such signalboxes every few miles or so. The job of the signalman is to accept a train from the box in the rear, get acceptance for it from the box ahead and then signal it forward. Each train is processed individually and passed on from box to box. The work demands not only mental alertness but physical fitness too.

In mechanical signalboxes signalmen pull heavy levers to work individual points and signals by means of rods, bars and wires. There is an 'interlocking frame' below the working floor. This is cleverly designed to prevent a signalman making mistakes. If he has signalled one train into a platform he cannot work any signal which would permit a conflicting movement. The signal lever is locked and however hard he pulls he cannot move it. In the signalbox also are block instruments and bells. Signalmen communicate to adjacent boxes by bell codes and by block instruments which read 'normal', 'line clear' and 'train on line'. These indications repeat themselves in boxes to the rear so there is always a record of the state of the line in each section. A section is the stretch of line between one signalbox and the next. Signals worked by the older boxes are often semaphore arms on the top of signal posts.

The basic idea of signalling is to divide the railway line into sections each controlled by a signalbox. Signalboxes are sometimes called 'block posts' because they control the passage of trains into the section ahead. The detailed rules which signalmen must observe are known as the Block Regulations. Signalling is a very technical subject and we will not be able to go into great detail in this specialist area. However, it is worth covering the rudiments of signalling.

There are different sets of Block Regulations which signalmen can apply. He knows which of these actually applies at any location because it is clearly laid down. The first system of signalling is covered by what is known as the Absolute Block Regulations. This provides for the strict separation of trains, with only one train being allowed in any section at a given time. This is the normal signalling system for passenger routes with mechanical signalboxes. There is another system called Permissive Block Working, usually found on goods lines. This does allow trains to enter an occupied section at slow speed after certain precautions have been taken.

On single lines over which traffic must pass in both directions, other regulations are in force. The Electric Token Block System is designed to prevent more than one train being in a block section at the same time. It achieves this by ensuring that the driver of every train carries a physical authority to proceed, known as a 'token'. These tokens are issued by the signalmen at each end of the section. They are removed by the signalmen from 'token instruments' in the signalbox. Only one token can be out of the machines at any one time and if a token is withdrawn at one end of the single line it locks the machine and signals at the other end so that no conflicting movement can possibly be authorised.

Signalmen in mechanical signalboxes use their block instruments and bells to communicate with each other and control the passage of trains by obtaining an acceptance from the box ahead that it is safe to signal a train forward.

This process is the basis of signalling. After satisfying himself that the block instrument reads 'normal' a signalman calls the attention of the signalman at the box ahead by means of the 'call attention' bell signal (one beat of the bell). When this is acknowledged by repetition, he asks if the line ahead is clear for a particular train. He identifies the class of train by another bell code. For example, to ask if the line is clear for an Inter-City express he gives four beats of the bell. If it is safe to do so, the signalman ahead can then repeat this bell signal back to accept the train, putting his block instrument to 'line clear'. This entitles the first signalman to place his signals in the 'off' position authorising the train to proceed. As the train enters the forward section the 'train entering section' bell code (two beats) is sent forward. On receiving this bell code the signalman ahead alters his block

74

instrument to 'train on line'. Like all block instrument readings, this message is repeated in the box to the rear, so both signalmen have a perfect understanding of the 'state of the line'. After the train has passed his signals, and entered the section ahead, the signalman replaces his signals to 'danger'. Once the train has gone through the section and arrived at the box ahead, the signalman there can send the 'train out of section' bell code (two-one) and put his block instrument for that line to 'normal'. The signalmen concerned have dealt with one train and are now ready to deal with the next one.

This is a very simple account of the way in which signalmen accept trains. There are variations to suit local or special circumstances, and signalmen are trained to know exactly what to do in all circumstances. The Block Regulations, the Rule Book and other operating instructions provide detailed procedures for signalmen on how to cope with every possible kind of emergency and under conditions of equipment failure.

It is not very often that signalmen have to apply emergency regulations but they need to be highly trained so that they do the right thing instantly. Without going too much into detail, it is worth noting that there are special procedures and emergency bell codes to cover a range of contingencies. These include 'obstruction danger', 'train divided', 'trains running away' in either direction, 'stop and examine' and other such matters. In addition there are special procedures for working over single lines when one line of double track is obstructed and for going to the assistance of a train which has broken down in a section. It all adds up to a fascinating job. To be a signalman you would need to be able to understand and absorb detailed working rules and apply them strictly.

Working in panel boxes

Like other railway administrations, the British Railways Board has been progressively modernising its signalling system. It has introduced a series of schemes to replace older mechanical equipment by new panel boxes. Signalling modernisation schemes tend to replace large numbers of mechanical boxes by a single panel box. For example, the Bristol panel box replaced 69 conventional boxes and employs 32 signalmen in place of 276 who were formerly employed.

The first thing you would notice if you went from a mechanical signalbox to a panel box would be the complete change of environment. The signalmen are no longer alone in their draughty cabins pulling heavy levers, processing individual trains. Instead they are part of a team in an air-conditioned, push-button environment. They cannot usually see the trains as they pass. They work on display panels with coloured light indications covering very large areas. They have to consider not one train at a time, but a whole complex pattern of trains. At any one time there can be dozens of trains displayed on the panel.

Modern panel signalboxes cover extensive areas. In a typical 'NX route relay power box' the method of signalling and route setting is on the entrance-exit (NX) principle. The signalman can set up a long route involving many points and signals just by turning a switch and pressing a button at each end of the route concerned. The signals will be colour lights capable of showing red, yellow and green in 3-aspect systems and red, yellow, double yellow and green in 4-aspect systems. He has a diagram of the track layout. Sections of line occupied by a train appear in red lights and routes which are clear when set-up appear in white lights. Each train is identified by a code on the train describer. Once again safety is in-built, but this time it is the electronics which prevent the signalman from authorising conflicting movements.

The panel is programmed not to accept instructions which would put trains in danger of collision. If he tries to set up a route which would lead to a train crash, nothing happens when he presses the button. The signalman in a modern box must plan for many trains to work through his area, and his special skill is in regulating traffic to avoid delays. If a driver sees a red signal he must stop. If he sees a yellow or double yellow he must reduce speed. So the signalman is just as vital to the good timekeeping of trains as the driver.

Much of the signalling of trains takes place within the areas controlled by the panel signalmen. The element of communicating understandings between adjacent signalmen which featured prominently in the job of the signalman in the mechanical box is not such an important part of the panel signalman's job. It can apply at the fringe of the area, however.

The panel signalman is helped by many electronic aids including automatic signalling over some sections of plain line. He can follow the passage of trains on his route diagram identifying them on the train describers. Even so he has a complex set of regulations to work to, known as the 'Track Circuit Block Regulations'. They are called this because the routes concerned are fully track circuited. The presence of trains is detected because axles complete the circuit between the rails which in turn operates relays and other electronic equipment in the panel box.

Track circuiting replaces block instruments as a means of establishing the state of the line and permits the developments of electronic signalling systems. Under Track Circuit Block Regulations there are detailed procedures for coping with exceptional and emergency working. Most signals have telephones and the signalmen have to give direct instructions to drivers. For example, they can authorise drivers to pass defective signals at danger in accordance with the regulations. They must, of course, know what they are doing and be trained in the safety procedures which they must apply. A recent development involves the use of cab-signalbox radio which allows continuous contact between drivers and signalmen. This is one of the conditions for one-man operation of passenger trains. This system also allows the signalman access to the trains' public address systems.

To work successfully in a panel box signalmen need self-confidence, detailed knowledge of modern signalling practice, an ability to cope with complex problems and the kind of mentality that can adapt to a push-button control environment. Many panel boxes have posts for regulators whose job it is to consider the overall movement of trains of differing types and speeds. They ensure that trains are signalled in a sequence which avoids or minimises delay.

Headquarters jobs in operations

Railway administrative jobs are described in the next chapter. However, perhaps some brief mention should be made of those headquarters jobs concerned with railway operations. Station salaried staff often move into this type of work on promotion. Every Region has a Chief Operating Manager who runs a major department. Within this department can be found a train planning office. Train planners convert the commercial specifications of the passenger, freight and parcels businesses into detailed train plans. This covers the provision and allocation of resources such as locomotives, coaches and wagons. Equally important is the allocation of train crew and the production of diagrams. Timetable planning is a fascinating specialist area which is increasingly computer-aided. Operations planning offers a great deal of scope for significant computer applications involving both main frame computers and microprocessors.

Another headquarters operating role is concerned with current operations, with productivity trend performance, train punctuality and with 'trouble-shooting'. The Headquarters Control Office is a 'nerve centre' for current operations management, although direct operations is increasingly delegated to local levels where practicable.

The office also plans signalling new works, monitors safety, oversees the application and development of detailed rules and regulations and other operating instructions.

The clerical and managerial grade structure will be described in the next chapter. At this stage it is sufficient to recognise that there are a wide range of clerical, managerial and planning posts concerning railway operations and that no account of the Operations function would be complete without some reference to this.

6 Railway jobs — technical, engineering and administrative

In this chapter we will be looking at the kind of work which can be found in the three major Engineering Departments of British Rail, and at the clerical and management activities which make up railway administration.

The Civil Engineering Department

British Rail is responsible for fixed assets on a scale which exceeds that of any other transport operator in the country. Most transport operators only have to worry about their mobile assets, such as lorries and buses, and not the road system over which they run. Similarly, a man driving his family car along a road thinks about the car as belonging to himself as owner-driver, and the road system as something which is just 'out there to be used'. He does not have to worry about the cost of maintaining the road or building new motorways. Somebody else looks after that, although he does make a contribution through taxation.

The situation on railways is quite different. Not only does British Rail own the rolling stock it owns the track too. This is an important asset. The railway system provides a network of routes which nobody else can use. It can be kept free of the sort of traffic jams and congestion you will find on busy roads and in large cities. But because they own the track, British Rail have to maintain it too. That also goes for all of the bridges, tunnels, buildings and other structures that make up the fixed assets of the railway system. Civil Engineering is, therefore, a major department in British Rail and many railway jobs are concerned with the maintenance and renewal of the track (known as the 'permanent way' or PW for short) and structures. The Civil Engineering Department has this important task.

The organisation of the Civil Engineering Department reflects railway geography. There are important activities taking place at Headquarters and in the Regions, but to get some idea about the kind of work done in the Department, we will look at one of the Divisions. A Civil Engineering Division will typically employ about

1500 staff, of which about 1200 would be directly concerned with the track itself. One such Division is located at Watford on the London Midland Region. It is managed by a Divisional Civil Engineer, who has two Assistant Engineers covering Permanent Way and Works respectively. They are supported by about 20 management staff, 50 technical staff and 50 clerical staff. The 1350 wages grade staff are controlled by about 100 supervisors. The Watford Division covers the very busy main line from Euston to beyond Rugby, the Midland Main Line from St. Pancras to Bedford, the Watford-Broad Street-North London line 'third rail' system and the Marylebone suburban routes.

Permanent way maintenance
Trackmen, Leading Trackmen and Track Chargemen
The biggest job to be done is day-to-day track maintenance of these routes. The Watford Division is typical of a large Civil Engineering Division. Track work is organised into 12 supervisors' sections, each of which has a number of 'permanent way gangs' on maintenance work. Each PW gang will have between 8 and 14 members. It is led by a Track Chargeman, who is responsible for work and performance and quality of maintenance. He is supported by three Leading Trackmen. One will be his deputy (known as the 'sub-ganger') while the others will be 'patrolmen'. Patrolmen walk the route and inspect the track. On high speed, high density routes this can be four times a week. On little used freight-only lines it could drop to once a week. The rest of the gang are Trackmen. Much of the work is quite heavy—shovelling ballast for example, but there are various items of small plant available. Routine trackwork is concerned with checking sleeper conditions, digging out and tidying up.

You join the wages grades on the track either as a Junior or a Probationary Trackman. You have to pass a trackman's course to qualify. In the PW maintenance gangs you have to pass skill tests to become a Skilled Trackman, Skilled Leading Trackman or Skilled Track Chargeman. Skills are re-tested every two years. You must pass these tests to retain the skill differentials, although you are allowed to re-sit twice after failure before being put back to the basic grade. Promotion is dependent on passing courses. Within the skilled grades of Leading Trackman and Track Chargeman there are different payments to reflect the range of responsibilities. The skill tests are the only means of progress from the basic to the skilled grades. Track knowledge and handsignalman's duties are always tested, but other tests are optional and include knowledge of particular equipment and procedures.

Maintaining the railway track is extremely important for safety of train running and to avoid delays. Each length of track is regularly and systematically checked for faults. Minor repairs are done on the spot. Special track testing vehicles can be attached to trains. Theser are fitted with special equipment which can produce a print-out from which the engineers can assess the condition of the track and plan remedial work.

Track work involves being out-of-doors in all weathers. In the very worst weather conditions, when there is ice and falling snow, permanent way staff are likely to be needed out on the ground clearing ice and snow from points and preventing the mechanical apparatus from freezing up. Some help is available from gas or electric point-heaters, but much manual work is still needed in these conditions. To work on the track you need to be fit and capable of heavy manual work where necessary. There is a lot of weekend and shift work involved, since the reduced train service on Sundays and at night permits easier access to the tracks for maintenance and renewal.

On track machinery
Machine Operators and Supervisors

Some of the track maintenance is done by sophisticated special-purpose machines. For example the Watford Division has 6 tamping and lining machines which cost about £¼ million each. These are used to correct the level and alignment of the rails and consolidate the ballast. Good quality track needs good 'top and line' as we call it. Each machine is operated by a team consisting of a supervisor and two machine operators. Unlike routine maintenance which is mostly done 'between trains' mechanised track maintenance needs 'absolute possession' whereby the engineer is given sole use of the line in question. Sometimes this can be done by 'weaves' where trains are diverted to running on adjacent lines.

With the increasing mechanisation of trackwork, there is a special group of grades concerned with the operation of the various machines which are used in the maintenance of railway track. There are three categories of Track Machine men, depending on the type and complexity of the equipment used. For example off-track machines are Category 3. Operators are trained to operate all machines in a particular pay group and are given skill tests.

Railway jobs—technical, engineering and administrative
Safety
Track workers need to remember that modern trains run up to 125 mph and there may not be much time to react to the approach of a train. There are very strict rules to protect track workers. First of all, each gang must have a 'lookout man' whose sole job is to warn of the approach of trains. You are then required to move to a place of safety. If you step aside onto another line you could get struck by a train coming the other way. The noise of the first train could prevent you hearing the second.

You must be safety-conscious and follow the rules if you work on the track. It is a dangerous place to work unless you do this every time, as a matter of routine. If the rules are followed then the job is perfectly safe. A train takes a mile to stop. If the driver sees you standing on the track in front of him and looking the other way, he cannot stop in time. Neither can he swerve to avoid you like a car. If you are a careless kind of person, not too happy about the idea of obeying rules designed for your own safety then keep off the track. We don't want you.

Track Chargemen
Track Chargemen must have a good knowledge of the Rules and Regulations which govern BR and must implement these rules in carrying out their task. They are responsible for ensuring that the job is completed as quickly as possible and minimising risk to staff. It is a responsible job. You need to be fit, alert and safety-conscious to work on the track.

Welding and ultrasonic testing
Track Welders
Each Civil Engineering Division has specialist trained welding staff for track work. There is a range of skills from basic thermal welding to arc welding. Track welding is important work. After training in gas cutting, jointing, bonding and metal arc welding trainees are appointed to be Track Welders. After further training and testing including electric arc welding by automatic process they can progress to a higher skill category. Track welders are paid at Track Chargeman rates. Ultrasonic testing is done to locate rail defects, diagnose faults and propose remedies.

Permanent way renewal
Trackmen, Leading Trackmen and Track Chargemen
In addition to the routine day-to-day maintenance, it is necessary to renew track periodically. This can be full relaying, which will

take place every 15-30 years depending on the category of track, or it can be re-ballasting. Relaying is done by relaying gangs each of 15 men. Unlike maintenance gangs who stick to their own patch, relaying gangs follow their work. The work arises as a result of the planned relaying programme. Each gang comprises a Track Chargeman, a Leading Trackman and 13 Trackmen. Because a lot of this work takes place at weekends, these men have special conditions of service which require them to work up to 40 weekends a year. If you are not prepared to accept this arrangement you will not be employed on PW renewal work.

The renewal work can involve specialist equipment, such as ballast cleaning machines, single jib rail cranes, single line gantries or track relaying machines which can take out and replace track panels. Modern track includes continuous welded rails on concrete sleepers.

Works

The other side of Civil Engineering is Works. This is concerned with the safety of bridges and structures. Bridges and Structures Examiners regularly report on the condition of bridges and structures, and these have to be maintained in a safe condition. There are jobs for plumbers, metal workers, bricklayers and carpenters on the works side of civil engineering.

Technical jobs in civil engineering
Junior Technical Officers, Technical Officers, Senior Technical Officers and Principal Technical Officers

In the Headquarters and Divisional drawing offices there are a range of interesting posts for technical staff. These are office-based jobs, although there is opportunity to visit sites on the ground. The normal entrant to Junior Technical Officer or Technical Officer would normally need 4 'O' level passes including English and Maths, preferably with a science subject also. Promotion is to Senior Technical Officer and then Principal Technical Officer. Higher rates of pay go to those with ONC or HNC qualifications. These jobs can be in PW or Works activities and can involve planning, renewals or maintenance. Typical work would include technical surveys, drawing and plotting re-alignments, preparing new works or bridge repair schemes.

There are many roadworks which impact on railway lines and there is a need to design new bridges for example to replace old ones. The track layout itself needs redesign and simplification to meet changing needs and reduce maintenance costs. Specific schemes are developed from concept to implementation. This is indoor work and can be fascinating for those with a technical bent. Technical Officers are trained for promotion. They get day release for TEC Civil Engineering Courses. Some are selected for indenture training and obtain a nationally recognised qualification in Civil Engineering as 'engineering technicians' or 'technician engineers'. This helps them progress to STO and PTO positions with an opportunity to progress into middle management.

The Department has wide ranging management opportunities for suitably qualified staff at Headquarters, in the Regions and in the Divisions. It is at Divisional level that direct responsibility for track and structures can be found. Each Civil Engineering Division is managed by a Divisional Civil Engineer who will be supported by experts on permanent way, bridges and structures. Ultimately the responsibility for the condition of the track and safety of the line in engineering terms lies on those who have engineering management responsibility. The Divisional Civil Engineers have personal responsibility for the track and structures which they maintain. With thousands of miles of track, numerous bridges and tunnels, British Rail employ many engineers.

The physical railway is sometimes called the 'infrastructure'. Unless this is sound it is impossible to run trains safely. So the Civil Engineers are an essential part of running a safe and punctual train service, even though they have nothing to do with the actual running of trains. The faster and more frequent the trains, the higher the engineering standards required, the more work needs to be done on maintenance and the greater the cost. For this reason the bulk of Civil Engineering work takes place on the main line Inter-City route network.

The Signal and Telecommunications Engineering Department

The second of the major engineering departments is the Signal and Telecommunications Engineering Department. It is the role of this Department to design, install, maintain and renew railway signalling and telecommunications equipment. Maintenance and construction work is usually kept separate to be done by different gangs. The Headquarters' role is concerned with strategy and planning rather than day-to-day installation or maintenance.

Signal engineering
The S & T Engineering Department is responsible for the installation and maintenance of signalling equipment. You will

recall that the actual operation of signalboxes is an operating job done by signalmen. Obviously those who operate the equipment need to work closely with those who maintain it.

On the signalling side, mechanical engineering was once dominant but increasingly the work involves combinations of electronic, light current electrical and mechanical engineering with various computer applications. New installations on main lines are mostly modern 'push button' colour light signalling systems with electronic train describers. Radio signalling techniques are also being developed for rural railways. The failure of a large modern panel signalbox could paralyse a significant part of the railway network. The work can involve shiftwork. It means working out-of-doors and it usually means working in small groups. In recent years the design of railway signalling systems has undergone great changes and the 'state of the art' is always developing.

Telecommunications engineering
The S & T Department provides engineering expertise in the communications field. British Rail has a completely automatic private telephone network with modern trunk exchanges covering the whole country and a telecommunications network linking railway offices, stations and depots. The transmission equipment operates over paired, fibre optic, coaxial and microwave links. BR has large integrated passenger information systems at major stations, fixed and mobile radios and closed circuit television installations. As computers are used increasingly there is a demand to provide communication links between computer terminals and between computer terminals and mainframe computers.

Throughout the country there are about 18 important centres where S & T Engineers have been established. Each Divisional Engineer has responsibility for signalling equipment, both maintenance and works. He also has responsibility for telecommunications equipment, both maintenance and works.

As an example of a large S & T Division we can take the Divisional S & T Engineer at Crewe. He has extensive route responsibilities which include parts of the West Coast Main Line, the North Wales route to Holyhead and the Welsh rural railways West of Shrewsbury. Because of this geographical spread he has signalling maintenance staff in about 20 locations and installation staff in 6 locations. A current major project is the new Chester Panel Box installation.

Railway jobs — technical, engineering and administrative

On the maintenance side the tasks can range from keeping a superb modern electronic installation in full working order to extending the working life of old-fashioned mechanical signal-boxes. Some of these can be regarded as working museums of Victorian technology. The more complex electronically controlled panel equipment tends to be maintained by more senior staff than the lineside equipment and conventional mechanical signalling equipment.

Entry into the S & T Department is either into the artisan wages grade posts, or into drawing office posts as trainee design staff.

Wages grade staff
The wages grade posts are described below, with a broad indication of the qualifications and duties:

GRADE	QUALIFICATIONS AND DUTIES
Railman	The entry grade for wages staff.
Assistant Technician	Must pass S & T test. Member of construction and installation group or helping to maintain equipment.
Tradesman/Installer	Trade qualifications or must pass S & T test. Acts as tradesman or assists on electrical and mechanical installation work. He is essentially a builder not a maintenance man.
Technician	Must pass S & T test. Responsible for his own maintenance section or assists Technical Officer or cable joiner. For example he could head a maintenance gang in conventional signalling areas such as those found on Welsh rural lines or assist on more complex modern equipment.
Leading Installer	Must pass S & T test. Responsible for the work of general purpose construction gang or installation group. For example this could involve installing new signals, level crossing barriers, or cable routes.
Senior Technician	Must pass S & T test. Responsible for his own maintenance section, or in charge of the installation of complex equipment. For example, this could be the outdoor equipment, mostly electrical, associated with panelboxes.

Technician Officer   ONC Engineering or City and Guilds.
Practical experience. Must pass S & T test.
Responsible for the maintenance of a
major installation with complex electrical
and electronic equipment including fault
diagnosis and testing. For example, this
could be the panel and train describers in
a major power signalbox or a large telecommunications centre. It requires a high
level of competence in electronics.

The skills and knowledge required for these posts are obtained on
structured courses mounted in the Regions or at the Railway
Engineering School, Derby. On the maintenance side the work is
usually done by small groups of three men. The composition of
gangs varies. Typical would be gangs consisting of a Senior
Technician, a Technician and an Assistant Technician. Alter-
natively a gang could have a Technician, an Assistant Technician
and a Railman.

The installation gangs on the works side are larger than the
maintenance gangs already described. They are typically 6-10
people, led by a Senior Technician for electrical work or a
Leading Installer for mechanical work. Other members of the gang
are Tradesmen/Installers and Assistant Technicians. Some HGV
drivers are also employed. Trainee technicians are expected to
take an approved TEC course. On starting they must opt for either
signalling or telecommunications. Initially they can perform either
installation or maintenance tasks.

Technical staff
There are 6 major centres in the country where design office work
is done for S & T Engineering. Design staff work in a drawing
office environment, although they do get the chance to do site
surveys and can get involved in commissioning and testing work.
Design office staff work on layout diagrams, circuit and wiring
diagrams, control tables giving electrical logic tables and, less
frequently these days, mechanical interlocking tables.

There is a need to analyse and record detailed technical
information and to provide a check on the design work which has
safety implications. There is a distinction between design work
which is done in the office and subsequent installation done by
artisan staff. The technical design staff are placed in four grades
which are briefly described below:

Railway jobs—technical, engineering and administrative

GRADE	BRIEF OUTLINE OF DUTIES
Junior Technical Officer *Technical Officer*	The design of signalling or telecommunications as part of a team in a drawing office. For example on electrical circuit design
Senior Technical Officer	The design of more complex signalling or telecommunications equipment and associated planning work.
Principal Technical Officer	The design of special or complex signalling or telecommunications equipment. Responsible for directing the work of others and checking its quality.

In addition the Department has its supervisory, administrative and managerial staff. S & T Engineering is an important aspect of railway engineering of which the general public have less awareness than other more visible elements in the railway business.

The Mechanical and Electrical Engineering Department

This is the third of major Engineering Departments. The work of the M & E Department is concerned with the mechanical and electrical components of locomotives, multiple units and railway rolling stock. The Department is also in the 'power supply' business where electrified lines operate. In addition the Department looks after railway plant and machinery. The work ranges from technical specification and design on one hand, to responsibility for the performance and maintenance of locomotives and rolling stock. Most jobs in the department involve direct contact with locomotives, carriages, wagons or other railway equipment. The kind of people who will be interested in this work will be those who have mechanical aptitude and enjoy car maintenance, or have an interest in electrical engineering. There is a wide range of both mechanical and electrical equipment to be designed and maintained. If you meet this requirement it is likely that you will already have a reasonable idea about the components of a locomotive and how they work.

The Mechanical and Electrical Engineering Department of a Region is headed by a Chief M & E Engineer, supported by senior engineers concerned with traction, rolling stock, electrification and plant. Important technical design and management activities are performed at this level.

However, it is at the ground level of the organisation that the actual depot work is performed and this is where many people seeking to join the railway industry would look for their first jobs. As an example of this depot work, we can take the activities controlled by the Area Maintenance Engineer at Willesden. This work covers four major activities. These are Traction Maintenance, Rolling Stock Maintenance, Electrification and Plant Maintenance and Technical Support.

Traction maintenance

The maintenance philosophy of the Department is 'planned preventive maintenance'. It is always better to avoid locomotive failures in traffic than to cope with emergency breakdowns. Planned preventive maintenance is based on agreed frequencies for all components based on time or use.

Within the Willesden area electric and diesel main line locomotives are maintained at the Traction Maintenance Depot.

Diesel locomotives Diesel power units go up to 3250 horsepower. These engines can have up to 16 cylinders with pistons as big as 10 inches in diameter. Diesel locomotives such as the Class 47 weigh-in at around 117 tons.

Each diesel locomotive is a mobile power station. It uses its diesel engine to drive a generator or alternator to provide electric power. Electrical and mechanical systems are used to control the power output of the engine. In the latest types there is electronic control of power output through 'thyristor chopper circuits'.

Many diesel locomotives are turbo-charged. As in Formula 1 motor racing, turbo-charging gets more power from smaller engines. Locomotives carry their own cooling systems and compressors. Traction motors on the locomotive bogies re-convert electrical power to mechanical power at the wheels.

Electric locomotives The power units of AC electric locomotives are transformers taking 25 kilovolts from the overhead wire through a pantograph mounted on the roof of the vehicle and converting it down to approximately 1000 volts. The current is rectified to DC for use in the traction motors.

The type of work which arises on both types of locomotives is examination, planned preventive maintenance and work arising. Work can arise from mechanical or electrical failures in service. This in turn may reflect a design problem needing modification, misuse of equipment, or maintenance problems. Major work is done at BREL Works but depots can themselves do any work on a diesel locomotive which does not require the engine to be removed. Depots can replace pistons and cylinder heads, turbo-chargers, pumps, valves, traction motors and other components. Similarly on electric locomotives depots can do most work 'in situ' which does not entail removing the transformer.

In the Willesden Area electric multiple units are also maintained at Croxley Electric Traction Depot and wagons at Stonebridge Park Wagon Shops. There are two types of electric multiple unit (EMU). One type take 25 kilovolts through the pantograph from the overhead system, transforming and converting it to DC for supplying the traction motors mounted on the bogies. The other type collects current through a pick-up shoe from a 650 volt DC conductor rail mounted outside the running rails and feeds the traction motors direct. Main line coaches are maintained in Willesden Carriage Shed. Modern passenger rolling stock is quite sophisticated containing air-conditioning systems for example. In order to achieve high levels of availability for traffic a system of modular maintenance operates. Defective components are removed for repair and replaced by new units.

Plant and machinery
A section of the staff deal with the maintenance of railway fixed plant and machinery. This covers the full range of equipment needed to run maintenance depots, cranes, on-track machinery and services such as heating and lighting.

The overhead line
Staff based at Willesden maintain the electrified overhead wires between Euston and Tring. The route is patrolled and maintained to give consistency of height and position. Some components with a limited life, such as electrical insulators, are periodically replaced. Damage to overhead wires can come about through birds, vandalism, accidental damage or due to the passage of trains, particularly if there is pantograph damage. Any damage results in a short circuit recorded in the Control Room where electric current distribution staff can control the supply pattern from the various sub-stations, switching if necessary. Similar work takes place on the third rail 650 volt DC system on the Watford to Broad Street route.

Wages grade posts

Once again there are different routes into employment in the Department. The first of these is to join the wages grade posts concerned with rolling stock examination and maintenance or with maintenance of the overhead line system. These are described below:

Rolling stock maintenance

GRADE	BRIEF OUTLINE OF DUTIES
Rolling Stock Technician	The basic work of rolling stock technicians is to examine passenger and freight stock out in the yards to establish its mechanical condition and fitness to continue in traffic. They can carry out small items of maintenance arising from minor defects. More experienced rolling stock technicians take on additional responsibility for higher grade work such as out-station preventive maintenance. There is some scope for those who have developed skills to transfer to workshop staff. Increasingly carriage and wagon maintenance work is performed in depots by workshop staff, rather than in yards and sidings.

Overhead line maintenance

GRADE	BRIEF OUTLINE OF DUTIES
Senior Lineman	Responsible for carrying out the maintenance, modification, installing, commissioning, renewal, earthing and bonding of the overhead power system. Dealing with incidents, reporting defects and taking charge of possessions on the track.
Lineman	Assists in the above work. When trained in certain skills and working methods, linemen can take on more responsible work at a higher rate of pay.

Railway jobs—technical, engineering and administrative

Workshop grades

In the maintenance depots of the M & E Department can be found a number of workshop jobs. Typical of them would be the following:

GRADE	BRIEF OUTLINE OF DUTIES
Craft Apprentice	4 year apprenticeship leading to skilled employment as a Category 4. Apprentices receive both on-the-job and off-the-job training to Engineering Industry Training Board requirements. Experience is given in both mechanical and electrical aspects.

Railway workshop staff

Railway Workshop Staff are placed in 4 categories. At one time there were about 200 separate job titles in railway workshops (fitter, trimmer, painter, metal machinist, welder, angle straightener, coach finisher II, chain examiner, wagon lifter, furnaceman, steam raiser, checker, slinger, traverserman, axle pad coverer, sandmixer, storesman etc. to name just a few). These days all of these separate jobs have been grouped together into the 4 categories. The basic definitions are as follows:

GRADE	BRIEF OUTLINE OF DUTIES
Railway workshop staff Category 1	Work which can be carried out by staff requiring limited experience or training, for example basic labouring, shed cleaning and materials handling jobs
Railway workshop staff Category 2	Duties which require staff to have the ability to assist others engaged in skilled work, in the operation of simple equipment. For example he can act as an assistant to a craftsman, working alongside a skilled man, say as a fitter's mate.
Railway workshop staff Category 3	Work of a lesser skilled character which does not call for closely defined limits, standards or finish. For example semi-skilled work changing brake blocks and brake pads on rolling stock, battery maintenance and simple electrical work.

Railway workshop staff
Category 4

Skilled work which demands a standard of competence needing a trade apprenticeship, or where a person is sufficiently competent and experienced to be capable of producing work to the standards specification or finish expected of a skilled employee. Fitters and electricians in traction maintenance and outdoor machinery depots can be dual-trained and qualify for a craft interchangeability allowance.

Within these broad bands detailed specifications of standards and qualifications appropriate to each category are defined for groups such as painters, storekeepers and welders. The allocation of work is the responsibility of Chargehands who report to Workshop Supervisors.

It is possible for staff to progress through the categories to Category 4 in some circumstances based on competence and experience. This occurs mainly on the carriage and wagon side. In traction maintenance depots Category 4's are normally apprentice-trained. BR trains its own apprentices and has a very good record of retaining them in railway employment subsequently.

Examples of skilled work in maintenance depots would include 'setting up' DMUs, refitting pistons, cylinder heads, turbo-chargers, etc, the testing and overhaul of brake valves and equipment, the examination and repair of control equipment and auxiliary contacts, the examination of traction motors and electrical equipment, changing components, setting-up equipment and testing

continued overleaf

93

BRIEF OUTLINE OF DUTIES
equipment. Typical trade skills would
be fitter, electrician, vehicle-builder,
plumber and welder. There is
provision for a measure of craft-
interchangeability when dealing with
mechanical and electrical
maintenance.

Workshop supervisory staff
The supervision of workshop staff is done by workshop supervisors who are themselves usually drawn from Category 4 skilled men. There are four supervisory grades reflecting different levels of responsibility.

Technical staff
The M & E Department employs Technical Officers, Senior Technical Officers and Principal Technical Officers in design office or technical support roles, similar to the arrangements already described for the other engineering activities.

Management in M & E Engineering
Management posts are open to suitably qualified staff in the Department, usually by promotion from those holding senior technical positions. There are opportunities for graduates who are either recruited from university or awarded an engineering sponsored studentship. The key management posts require professional engineering qualifications.

British Rail Engineering Limited
British Rail Engineering Limited (BREL) is one of the largest engineering concerns in the country, building locomotives and rolling stock for BR and export and also carrying out heavy maintenance of locomotives and rolling stock. BREL is a wholly owned subsidiary of the British Railways Board.

It has 13 major workshops at Crewe, Derby(2), Shildon, Doncaster, Wolverton, Temple Mills, York, Swindon, Ashford, Eastleigh, Glasgow and Horwich. Currently there is a review to determine the future workshop capacity required. Its Head-quarters is in Derby where the Railway Technical Centre is also to be found. BREL is in full scale production of power cars and Mark III coaches for the Inter-City 125 trains, Class 58 diesel electric freight locomotives, electric multiple units and high capacity air-braked wagons. The range of jobs available in BREL is typical of that found in heavy engineering with almost every skilled craft being represented. In employment terms BREL should be regarded as directly comparable to any heavy engineering activity rather than as an activity which is peculiar to railway work. They just happen to be making locomotives rather than electrical generators. However, if you are interested in railways, you may feel that you would prefer to work in an industry which manufactures trains, rather than in one which makes other equipment. The grade structure in BREL is similar to that found in the Regional traction maintenance depots described earlier.

As an example of a major BREL works we could pick Crewe. This is a large works covering 90 acres. It is here that the power cars for the Inter-City 125 were built and here that main line electric and diesel locomotives are built and shopped for major repairs. A tour of the works would acquaint us with the main activities on the site. These include the Steel Foundry, the Wheel Shop, the Cubicle Shop, the Heavy Machine Shop, the Plate Fabrication and Welding Shops, the Electric Locomotive Erecting Shop, the Locomotive Test Centre, the Diesel and Electric Locomotive Repair Shop, the Power Unit and Bogie Repairs Shop, the Auxiliary Motor Repair Shop, the Copper Shop, the Bogie Repair Shop, the Chain Shop, the Smithy, the Signal Shop, the Steam Generator Repair Shop, the Brass Shop, the Stores, the Amenity Block and the offices. If you want to know more about them, you should try and pay a visit to the Works on one of its well-known Open Days.

At present Crewe Works has over 400 apprentices. About half of these are fitters, but there are also electricians, machinists, platers, coppersmiths, sheet metal workers, welders, painters, patternmakers, moulders, leather-workers, smiths and joiners.

The Grade structure for railway workshop staff is similar to that described for the maintenance workshops. Examples are given below of the kind of work found in BREL within these grades:

GRADE	BRIEF OUTLINE OF DUTIES
Railway workshop staff Category 1	Labouring and Storesmen in the various shops around the works.
Railway workshop staff Category 2	Posts can include watchman, semi-skilled machinists, assistants to craft grades, checkers, crane drivers, truck drivers, semi-skilled painters, Bosch attendants, slingers, cleaners, coil winders and stores issuers.

Railway jobs—technical, engineering and administrative

GRADE	BRIEF OUTLINE OF DUTIES
Railway workshop staff Category 3	Posts can include crane drivers, semi-skilled machinists, shunters, stores issuers and dressers.
Railway workshop staff Category 4	These are skilled posts, mainly for apprentice-trained men, as fitters, electricians, welders, patternmakers, coppersmiths, platers, sheet metal workers, riveters, foundrymen, woodworkers, turners, smiths, bricklayers, metal machinists, painters, plumbers, plasterers, trimmers and storekeepers.

At the top is the Works Manager and his management team supported by works supervisors, professional and technical and clerical staff. The management structure is shown in the simplified chart below:

Works Manager

Quality Assurance Engineer — Production Manager — Technical Services Manager — Works Chief Accountant — Personnel and Admin. Officer — Works Supplie Officer

Production Engineers

Superintendents

Workshop Supervisors

It will be clear from this that BREL is an important employer in its own right, with a wide range of employment opportunities in the heavy industrial engineering field.

Administration: the management structure
In an organisation as large and complex as British Rail, there is an administrative and managerial role to play, above Area and Depot level. The British Railways Board has its Headquarters in London. There are five Regions, each with its own Headquarters offices. These are the London Midland Region at Euston, the Western Region at Paddington, the Eastern Region at York, the Southern Region at Waterloo and the Scottish Region at Glasgow.

Administrative work is of great variety. Staff are attached to departments such as Passenger, Freight, Parcels, Operations, Planning, Finance, Personnel, Management Services, Civil Engineering, Mechanical and Electrical Engineering, Signal and Telecommunications Engineering and several others of a more specialist character such as those dealing with medical, legal and architectural matters.

It would be quite impossible to give you a flavour of every job which is done, but perhaps it would illustrate the grade structure to describe some jobs at each of the levels in the grade structure. Staff with suitable qualifications and experience can, in competition with others, apply for posts higher up the scales. There are five grades of clerical officer posts and five grades of management staff posts. The samples below are taken from Area and Headquarters level. The clerical officer grades go from the basic entry grade of C.O.1 to the top clerical officer grade of C.O.5:

Clerical Officers—sample jobs at area level

GRADE	SAMPLE POST	BRIEF DESCRIPTION OF DUTIES
C.O.1	*Area Admin Clerk*	Ordering and distribution of stores and stationery. Maintenance of leave and sickness records. Distribution and despatch of correspondence, train service notices, etc.
C.O.2	*Area Roster Clerk*	Allocation of train crew, operations and other personnel to duty rosters; related deployment of 'relief' staff to cover leave, sickness, etc, absences.
C.O.3	*Area Clerk (Works, Accommodation & Stores)*	Correspondence, records, arrangements for contractors, etc, to undertake repairs to stations and buildings in Area. Related Health and Safety considerations.
C.O.4	*Area Clerk (Staff and General)*	Arrangements for recruitment, promotion and transfer of staff. Election procedure for staff representatives. Secretarial duties at negotiation or consultative discussions. Internal audit duties.
C.O.5	*Area Budget Clerk*	Budget compilation, monitoring of

continued overleaf

BRIEF OUTLINE OF DUTIES
results, analysis of trends, manpower
forecasts for one or more Area
Manager or Engineer.

Clerical Officers—sample jobs at regional HQ level

GRADE	SAMPLE POST	BRIEF DESCRIPTION OF DUTIES
C.O.1	HQ Finance	Filing and registration of correspondence. Preparation of stationery requisitions. Supervised assistance to others as required.
C.O.2	HQ Passenger	Collation of ticket statistics, etc, and preparation of information for meetings as directed.
C.O.3	HQ Operations	Assist with programming of locomotives, coaching stock and train crews—matching resources with the needs of the timetable.
C.O.4	HQ Personnel	Correspondence and telephone enquiries on conditions of employment from other BR Offices and Trade Unions, preparation of memoranda for discussion with TU and other Staff Representatives.
C.O.5	HQ Civil Engineering	Supervision of small group of staff; liaison with technical staff to arrange provision of materials for track renewal and maintenance, including correspondence with supply companies.

You will appreciate that this is merely a sample of posts in a complex administrative structure. Other office jobs are placed in the same grading system so that Audio Typists and Shorthand Typists are graded C.O.1 or C.O.2 and Secretaries are graded C.O.2 to C.O.5 depending on the level of their work.

Controllers

These are a specialist group of staff concerned with traffic control who have direct contact with stations and signalboxes. They continually monitor working performance and carry out remedial measures or contingency plans to overcome difficulties. These staff work in control offices and they have their own grading structure which covers five grades of controller.

Management
Above the clerical officers there are five grades of management posts, M.R.1 to M.R.5, ranging from junior management level to senior middle management. Once again it is only possible to give some sample posts by way of illustration.

Management staff—sample posts at area level

GRADE	SAMPLE POST	BRIEF DESCRIPTION OF DUTIES
M.R.1	Station Manager	Located at the larger stations. Responsible on a shift basis for overall supervision of day to day station activities.
M.R.2	Area Passenger and Parcels Manager	Responsible to an Area Manager for the operations, commercial and financial aspects of a geographical area containing a number of stations, yards etc. Support staff could include M.R.1 Station Managers for a large station, in addition to direct command lines to 'outbased' Assistants, who in turn have an overview of a number of small stations.
M.R.3	Area Personnel Officer	Responsible to one or more Area Managers and Engineers for all personnel and administration activities including staff relations, labour law, budgets, typing and reprographic facilities and accommodation matters.
M.R.4	Area Maintenance Engineer	Responsible for the maintenance of traction, rolling stock, fixed equipment, plant and machinery to specified standards with associated personnel and budget responsibilities.
M.R.5	Area Manager	Total responsibility for all operating and commercial activities —the railway business—in a geographical area, which will

continued overleaf

Continued

BRIEF OUTLINE OF DUTIES
include stations, signalboxes, yards
and the personnel and budget
responsibilities for them.

Management staff—sample posts at Regional HQ level

GRADE	SAMPLE POST	BRIEF DESCRIPTION OF DUTIES
M.R.1	Finance Assistant (HQ Finance)	Responsible for summarising and producing working results. Supervises the production of budget and outturn data. Analysis of financial trends.
M.R.2	Asst. Engineer (Standards) (HQ, M & EE)	Review and issue of maintenance and workshop overhaul schedules, related instructions and technical literature. Modification of locomotives.
M.R.3	New Works Design Engineer (HQ, CS & TE)	Organisation and administration of signalling projects and associated control planning and design work. Approval of signalling plans.
M.R.4	Assistant (Employee Relations) (HQ Personnel)	Advice and guidance on policy matters affecting conditions of employment, labour law and industrial disputes, negotiation and consultation with Trade Union and other Staff Representatives.
M.R.5	Planning Manager (Finance, Authorisation and General)	Preparation and monitoring of investment budget for resignalling and other projects. Liaison with technical and other departments—Contract, Parliamentary and Estate responsibilities.

You will understand that in a very large organisation there is a complex management structure and that these posts are merely samples to give some flavour of railway management posts.

Above this, at the very top, are the top jobs in the industry which comprise members of senior management, the senior executive group and finally the Board members themselves, including the Chairman and Chief Executive.

7 Getting in and getting on

As you would expect, there are quite a number of methods of entry to British Rail. Some methods of entry are in the form of training schemes aimed at school leavers or the young unemployed. You can also join British Rail by direct entry into a job. From the age of 18 onwards you can take up adult employment at adult rates of pay. If you are under 18 you will normally be a junior or a trainee of some kind. There is a scheme for recruiting 'A' level candidates and sponsoring them at University. In addition there are advanced training schemes aimed at those with University degrees or similar qualifications and internal candidates of high calibre.

You may have no formal qualifications. You may have some CSE grades. You may have passed some GCE 'O' or 'A' levels. Or you may even have a University degree. Whatever you have or have not, you can be sure that there is a method of entry for which you can be considered, and a prospect of a railway job for you. But a word of warning. Many of these methods of entry are competitive and depend on the availability of jobs. We would like you to consider a job on British Railways and we would like to feel that you could make it, but obviously we cannot make any promises. If you are interested I suggest you contact your nearest British Rail office. For more information about the advanced training schemes write to the British Railways Board, Rail House, Euston Square, London NW1 2DZ. For most railway jobs it would be best to contact your local office, the address and telephone number of which can be found in your local telephone directory.

Training schemes for school leavers
There are a number of special training schemes which are aimed at school leavers. These are described below:-

Craft Apprentices
BR offer four-year craft apprenticeships in line with that specified by the Engineering Industry Training Board. The training is in four stages. These are basic craft training, EITB modules in craft knowledge and skills and a railway module covering knowledge and skills. As part of your training you attend Technical College

101

following a suitable course such as City and Guilds Craft Certificate course in Mechanical and Electrical Engineering. Entrants are 16-17 years old. No specific qualifications are needed, but you should show an aptitude for practical engineering and be interested in mathematics and science. Apprentices who show special promise may be able to transfer to the training scheme for Railway Engineering Technicians. On completion of an apprenticeship you become eligible for the full craft rate of pay. Craft apprenticeships are available on the Regions in Mechanical and Electrical Engineering and Civil Engineering and also with British Rail Engineering Limited.

Railway Engineering Technicians, Trainee Signal and Telecommunications Technicians

Technicians are employed in each of the main branches of railway engineering—Civil Engineering, Signal and Telecommunications Engineering and Mechanical and Electrical Engineering. You need at least four GCE 'O' level passes or equivalents, including Maths, English and a Science subject. The training combines instruction, practical training and job experience. Day or block release is given for studying to obtain an ONC in Engineering or taking the City and Guilds Technician courses.

Traction Trainees

At the moment the way to join the railway if you want to become a driver is as a traction trainee. This scheme is open for school leavers between 16 and 18 years old and others up to the age of 22. You must be physically fit and have good eyesight and normal colour vision. Normally you will be expected to be 5 ft 2 in. tall at 16 or 5 ft 4 in. tall at 18. You are expected to be able to demonstrate that you have reached an acceptable standard in Maths, English and Science, although no formal educational qualifications are needed.

The first part of the training will cover all aspects of train working and railways rules and regulations. You will be trained in the duties of the Driver's Assistant. Drivers' Assistants can act as 'secondmen' in the cabs of trains or locomotives and operate the steam heating equipment where necessary. As single-manning is extended the number of Drivers' Assistants posts is likely to decline and this is why talks are going on to introduce a new grade of 'trainman' which will open up a new line of promotion for station staff and guards to become drivers. The present line of promotion is from Traction Trainee to Driver's Assistant and then to Driver.

102

You are not able to drive trains until you are 21 years old and have successfully completed the training. You must first gain sufficient experience as a Driver's Assistant and then satisfy an Inspector that you are competent in rules and regulations, that you understand timetables, signals of all types, braking systems and train formations. You must also have a full knowledge of the type of traction you will be driving and the routes over which you drive. You will also have to pass a practical examination covering driving techniques and train working. Drivers are given further training to extend their traction and route knowlege.

Junior Traffic Trainees

School leavers of 16-18 years of age can join as Traffic Trainees although the size of the intake may be restricted. After you have been a trainee for one year, provided you have reached 18, you can get an adult appointment as a railman, guard, shunter or signalman. The training will prepare you for the job of your choice. During your training you will have practical involvement in work at stations, marshalling yards, motive power depots, freight terminals and signalboxes. So you will get a good all round idea about basic railway work.

Junior Clerical Staff

School leavers who meet the educational qualifications or who can pass an entrance examination can be trained in various aspects of office work. This leads to clerical, administrative and managerial posts at stations or in headquarters' offices.

Youth Training Scheme

Railway training schemes are regarded by the Manpower Services Commission as a suitable bridge between school and work, to give training in job skills. Consequently British Rail will be participating in the Government sponsored Youth Training Scheme. Further information is available from careers advisers and local Job Centres.

Direct entry

For the older applicant who is not able to apply for the various training schemes, there is the possibility of direct entry into base-grade adult posts at the age of 18 or over. In the traffic grades the entry job is railman but recruits are often taken on with the intention of immediate training for more senior grades, such as guard, shunter or signalman. There are openings to join the

Getting in and getting on
maintenance gangs on the permanent way in the entry grade of Trackman. For clerical and administrative work there is direct recruitment into clerical officer positions at station, depot and headquarters levels.

Training schemes for 'A' level school leavers
Many 'A' level students join British Rail direct from school. Some join direct into clerical and administrative posts. If you do this you would hope that your qualifications would later help you compete successfully for promotion within the industry. If you proved that you could master your first job quickly they probably would. In addition to this direct entry, there are special training schemes aimed at 'A' level candidates for Supplies Management and Finance and Accountancy.

Sponsored engineering studentships
Each year British Rail sponsors a limited number of students on University sandwich courses which combine an honours degree course in engineering with practical engineering training on the railways. This can be in any branch of engineering. On completion of their training sponsored students are appointed to Senior Technical Officer posts in the engineering departments or BREL.

Advanced training schemes
British Rail has a long-standing interest in recruiting good University graduates into the railway industry. Quite a few University graduates join as ordinary recruits and hope to make their mark within the industry, as indeed do very many people without that kind of qualification. However, each year British Rail takes a limited number of graduates into its advanced training schemes. Graduate training is offered in electronic engineering, electrical engineering, operational research, computing, operations management, marketing management, personnel management, finance and accountancy management, retail and catering management and estate management.

These are all highly competitive schemes and the proportion of successful candidates is, therefore, very small in relation to the number of applicants. These schemes are open to suitably qualified internal candidates of good calibre who are selected to train alongside the graduate recruits. This takes place notably in operations management.

The new job

Anyone who takes on a job for the first time has some important adjustments to make. You will probably welcome your new status in the community and welcome the change from school or unemployment. You may have been an important person at school. As a senior pupil, younger school children would have noticed you, maybe looked up to you a bit. Age and experience were on your side. Suddenly you get your first job. What a change! Instead of being a senior person with a bit of status, you find yourself right at the bottom of the heap again. It is other people who have the age, the seniority, the knowledge and the experienece. You are just a raw recruit. With nothing to offer except your keenness. "Go and make us a cup of tea", they say, and off you go whether you like it or not! You may find you are given a lot of the routine mundane tasks at first. It is your job to get stuck in. Master the nuts and bolts and earn yourself the right to progress to the more interesting parts of the job.

You will also find that you need to adjust to the demands and responsibilities of work. You will be expected to come to work on time and do a full week's work. If you do not realise this you could quickly be in trouble, and you could even lose your job before you've hardly started. If your employer discovers you are unsuitable he will not be slow in getting rid of you, before your probationary period expires.

The world of work is much tougher than the world of school and you should appreciate this before you join it. Whatever the job you get, it will have duties and responsibilities laid down. You will be judged on how well you discharge these duties and responsibilities. There is pride and satisfaction to be derived in a job well done, especially in a service industry where you are there to help other people. Most railway jobs are of a kind where you can see the results of your work day-by-day, so you know if you are successful or not. It is good to achieve success in a job. It adds to job satisfaction. It can give real pleasure—rather like scoring a goal in football—especially if you win against the odds. I am not saying you will not meet the cynics, the grumblers, the moan-and-groan brigade and even those who do not enjoy their jobs! All I can say is that I know from experience that railway work can be fun and enjoyable if you give it your full commitment. If you can sustain your enthusiasm it will increase your chances of promotion and help you to enjoy the job more.

There are special demands of basic railway work—like being prepared to work awkward hours and shifts, and having to work out-of-doors in all weathers. You will also have to be very strict in safety matters. You may be expected to wear a uniform. If you deal with the public, your appearance, manner, behaviour and courtesy are important. With effort on your part and with discipline you can earn the respect of your colleagues and customers.

Application Forms and Job Interviews

I want to give you some advice. This is based on long experience of interviewing railway applicants at all levels, from school leavers up to University graduates. For most jobs you will be asked to complete an Application Form and attend for interview. It is important for you to realise that these are both very important and could have a real influence over whether you get the job or not.

The Application Form is your opportunity to 'sell yourself' to a potential employer. If it is untidy, incomplete or badly written, the person responsible for recruitment will lose interest in you. Some of the questions on the form may be simply factual. You are not going to score a big hit just by writing your name and address. But sometimes other questions can be asked, for example, why you want the job. These require more careful thought. Always give time and trouble to completing Application Forms properly. An employer will sometimes think that if an applicant cannot be bothered to fill a form up properly, why should he be bothered to interview him.

Interviews should also be seen as positive opportunities to sell yourself. It is the job of the good interviewer to put you at your ease. Do not be nervous. If you are keen on the job make sure you communicate that enthusiasm. Decide before the interview what you want to 'get across' and make sure you let the interviewer know about any relevant experience or interests you have.

Finally, if you turn up too casual or scruffy, or with a 'couldn't care less' attitude, you may find that the interviewer is not impressed. It is not that employers look for conformist 'yes sir, no sir' types, although some do. In fact they probably welcome some signs of spirit and independence. Certainly I always do. But you must 'put your best foot forward' at the interview if you want the job. It is really a question of attitude and many young people, who do not have much experience of interviews, reduce their own chances of getting a job by not thinking carefully enough about the interview process itself and how they plan to use it as an opportunity to press their claims for jobs.

Promotion prospects

Most railway promotion comes from within the industry and anyone who is prepared to acquire the training and experience needed can look forward to a progressive career. In wages grade positions seniority is an important factor in promotion, but you need to demonstrate you are suitable to do the job. In the salaried grades, covering clerical officers, supervisors and managers, posts are filled largely on the basis of suitability, although obviously seniority is a factor which is taken into account. It is the practice within BR for vacancy lists to be circulated amongst those who are entitled to apply for particular jobs. So you can apply for any job which interests you.

Since the railway is a geographically dispersed industry, jobs can occur all over the system. In the wages grades, vacancies for jobs are initially posted within agreed 'promotional areas'. By contrast management posts are advertised system-wide. Ambitious managers may need to be prepared to move their home to gain the promotion they want. This is helped by financial assistance in moving house. Many senior managers have worked in several parts of the country. British Rail takes trouble to ensure that its systems of promotion are fair to all concerned. Railways are large enough to offer very good career opportunities at all levels. Indeed it is still very possible to join BR 'at the bottom' and rise to a senior management position on hard work and merit.

8 Some typical days in the lives of railway people

In this chapter we will be looking at some typical days in the lives of railwaymen. These are real people who have given information about themselves. The comments quoted are selected from those which they made themselves.

Name   Colin Green   **Panel Box Signalman, Rugby**
Age   39
Length of service   24 years

Typical day
Colin Green says:
'I work a late shift in Rugby Panel Box from 1400 to 2200. This is a major modern panel box on the West Coast Main Line. I am responsible for controlling the movement of a hundred or so trains in the course of my shift. Most of this works smoothly according to plan, but today has its share of incidents. Two express trains have 'special stop orders' so they are signalled into the platform lines instead of the through lines. A guard reports experiencing a 'bump' on the Down line at Weedon. I arrange for the line to be examined by another train (1J33) and caution other trains in the section. Later the line is 'blocked' for a while so that a permanent way supervisor can carry out an inspection of the line. At the end of my duty I hand over to the night shift signalman to take over the panel.'

Feelings about the job
'I find Panel Box work interesting in that there is always something going on. Even the occasional emergencies are almost part of the routine, because I have the skill and experience to cope with them. nevertheless I feel that modern panel boxes lack the 'atmosphere' of the manual boxes, where the work was more physical, so that after a day on a busy box you went home tired. Sometimes at weekends I act as pilotman or signalling agent when engineering works are being carried out. It can be unpleasant being outside in the depth of winter but I appreciate the opportunity to see the working of the

railway on the ground in visiting parts of the district I would not normally see.'

Likes and dislikes

'I feel that my job is interesting and varied and that you can become addicted to railway work, especially signalling. Sometimes the responsibility can weigh heavily and late shift is not 'the greatest'. I think that there is a threat to the future of the railways which I find unsettling. In any case I believe that fewer staff will be needed in the signalling grades. I regret the passing of the old railway scene, with branch lines, country stations, manual boxes and semaphore signals. I see that sidings are lifted and loops taken out and that some lines could close. This saddens me.'

Name Alan Shufflebotham   **Chargeman, Stoke-on-Trent**
Age 23
Length of service 6½ years

Typical day
Alan Shufflebotham says:

'I arrive at work as rostered. I shunt the yard and when the Driver arrives I dispose of the wagons according to the TOPS computer lists. I prepare trains for departure. We take a supply of ferry wagons to the British Steel Corporation private sidings at Etruria. If required we do shunting at Etruria and dispose of loaded wagons from BSC by taking them back with our shunting engines from Etruria to Cockshute Yard at Stoke-on-Trent. This is followed by more shunting to dispose of wagons released from the yard for external movement.'

Feelings about the job

'I like working in all weathers. I feel I am more suitable for outside work and I have been issued with clothing for this kind of job.'

Likes and dislikes

'I like the greater responsibility given to the person in charge, and also the variety of work. I also like working in different areas. I have no complaints about working outside.'

Some typical days in the lives of railway people

Name Adrian Dent BSc, **Management Trainee (Marketing)**
Age 22
Length of service 5 months

Typical day
Adrian Dent says:

'There is no such thing as a typical day for a management trainee on this scheme. I have worked in London, Crewe, Watford, Liverpool, Warrington, Wigan, Nottingham, Birmingham and Manchester. I have worked days, nights, early and late turns. I have met many railway staff at all levels and as part of a project I had to interview top managers from Shell and ICI. Taking a sample day, I arrive at the Liverpool office at 0900 and prepare an interview questionnaire for ICI. At 1035 I leave by train for Runcorn where I have a meeting with the ICI Distribution Manager in connection with my project work. This includes lunch. Then it is back to Liverpool in the afternoon to write out the interview notes in detail and prepare questions for a costing and resources study in Trans-Pennine petroleum and chemical movements.'

Feelings about the job

'When I started to work for the railway my friends started to crack all the standard jokes. This begins to get to you and I was apprehensive about if I was doing the right thing. Now I am sure I am. Comparing notes with those who joined other companies I find they are often bored, over-worked, or doing menial tasks with very little of substance to get their teeth into.'

Likes and dislikes

'I like the variety and opportunity to meet different people at all levels in the organisation. There is a lot of change happening as BR becomes more commercial or market-orientated. This provides a great challenge. There is scope to work hard, have fun, introduce new ideas and rise or fall on their success. Sometimes the travelling gets very tiring and I wish I had more time at home. If you are allocated to someone who simply tells you how (not why) he does his job, it can get very boring.'

110

Some typical days in the lives of railway people

Name Norman Williams, **Clerical Officer, Booking Office, Stoke-on-Trent**

Age 57
Length of service 17 years

Typical day
Norman Williams says:

'On a typical day I enter the office at 0545 through three security doors, and check the cash 'float' from the previous turn. I prepare to distribute ticket issuing machines, floats and excess books to the Conductor Guards. I check the floats for the parcels office and for outstation excess book sales. I check the dates on all the machines and endorsing stamps. I empty cash from the platform ticket issuing machines. The total cash must balance the value of the tickets issued. I collect the monies left by the night ticket collector (excess ticket receipts) on security with the Station Supervisor. I check and debit this. I then release cash for float purposes to the second clerk to be reclaimed as soon as possible. Between 0545 and 0650 I book tickets generally before assuming responsibility for the main window (destinations A-L) from 0630-1200. This includes Group Party Bookings, Season Ticket issues and Special Ticket issues in addition to normal ticket sales. I receive, check and debit omniprinter receipts from the Collector Guards during my turn of duty. I receive and check excess fares monies from Travelling Ticket Inspectors. At 1200 I complete the accountancy part of my job by creating a 'balance' (credits and debits) for my turn of duty. I maintain a surveillance of the ticket stocks, ordering as required.'

Feelings about the job
'Whilst ticket issuing is routine, friction can occur with the passengers. For example if a train is about to depart and there is a queue of passengers at the Booking Office window I try and deal with immediate passengers in preference to someone at the front of the queue with a non-urgent transaction. He may object to this. When someone presents a pre-signed cheque, he may resent my request for a second signature as confirmation.

'A Booking Clerk is regarded as a talking timetable. Before the information office opens at 0845 the booking clerks deal with enquiries. When I am under pressure issuing tickets it is not always possible to look up timetables. A passenger may then ask sarcastically 'Too much trouble for you?' The small minority of these instances can nullify the innumerable

111

Some typical days in the lives of railway people

occasions when passengers express gratitude for assistance given. I honestly believe that less than 1% of the complaints are justified.'

Likes and dislikes

'I like the continued involvement of the job. There is no time for boredom. There is a strong cameraderie between all members of the staff with complete trust, confidence and willingness to assist under pressure. I dislike that fact that there is no facility for a static break for a sandwich. Eating whilst mobile is very unsatisfactory. There is an increasing number of cheques and credit cards tendered, causing delay. I have had as many as 100 in a single turn. A minority of passengers can be difficult or objectionable.'

Name   William McCartney   **Guard, Rugby**
Age   36
Length of service   8 years

Typical day

Bill McCartney says:

'For my typical day I have picked Turn 214. On this day I book on at 0850. After booking on I spend a few minutes checking the Late Notice Board. By this time my train has arrived. I depart at 0912 arriving at Euston at 1100. I keep the same unit (EMU) all day. I leave Euston at 1135 arriving at Milton Keynes at 1251. I have about 35 minutes here and I spend some of the time looking around the new station. I then depart at 1325 arriving Euston at 1439. We do not stop here long. I depart at 1459. This time is spent in sorting out Red Star parcels and anything else in my Brake Van. I get 5 minutes walking to the Booking on Point and 10 minutes tickets before I book off at 1705. For my typical day I picked a passenger turn. We also do a lot of freight work.'

Feelings about the job

'It is not the best of jobs in winter. For example in other jobs when it is raining you can stop work and shelter. But in my job it does not matter if it is raining or snowing a blizzard, I must go and prepare my train. This has to be done to keep the train running to time as much as possible. We are supplied with a uniform including leggings, so these keep you reasonably dry and warm.'

Likes and dislikes

'I like the fact that after booking on you are given your day's work, then allowed to get on with it without any supervision. If I was in a factory I would have a Foreman watching me all day. On this job you are trusted to get on with it. I am not so keen on some of the shifts, but as our service runs 24 hours a day this is something that goes with the job. Sometimes I spend too much time hanging around waiting for my train. This can be as much as four hours which can be very boring.

'I am also involved in industrial relations. For the last three years I have been the Secretary of the Local Departmental Committee. This is the forum for discussion between management and staff at local level.'

Name David Cullen,   **Signalman, Northampton No. 4 Box**
Age 53
Length of service 27 years
David Cullen has spent nearly all his working life in signalboxes. He has worked eighteen different boxes altogether.

Typical day
David Cullen says:

'Northampton No. 4 is a three shift signalbox manned continuously. On a typical day early turn I rise at 0445 and leave home at 0515 in order to arrive at work by 0550 in time to get my coat off and evaluate proceedings before taking over duty at 0600. I accept responsibility by 'signing on' in the Train Register. Work starts immediately with the signalling of through freight and passenger trains. I must get engines off empty passenger stock which involves 'running round' between signalboxes. I book each train movement and time in the Register. There is a lot of telephone contact concerning the working. I handle signal faults and failures and make alternative working arrangements with colleagues to cope with late-running. During a shift I need to cope with 60-80 trains. Sometimes the West Coast Main Line expresses are diverted via Northampton when this can go up to 140 trains a shift. In addition there are shunting moves. I have to provide protection for the PW Gangers and do overhead line isolations. This signalbox works three separate signalling systems (absolute block, track circuit block and permissive goods block) over different lines, each with its own set of regulations. Northampton No. 4 is a manual box with 85 levers in the frame.

113

Some typical days in the lives of railway people

During an early shift I will have to pull between 400 and 700 heavy levers.'

Feelings about the job

'I feel that running the railways is a team job. Each signalman is a part of that team. If we all did our part we should succeed and never forgetting that all grades are part of the team. Leadership and example must count. I do my small part and I hope it counts. The workload can vary from light traffic and quiet periods to being extremely hectic. Sometimes five phones can be ringing. If one is fully rested prior to work it is easier to handle. I believe in doing one's best and take pride in looking after the job. I am responsible for the safety of the travelling public and for avoiding delay. I try and work with all staff cheerfully. I will admit my faults and mistakes if they are mine, but not if I believed I was right. I feel sometimes that the railway expects more from signalmen than from other grades. I don't resent this but I feel we have been left behind in pay and conditions considering what we are expected to know and accept responsibility for. It is because we like the job that we stay in it.'

Likes and dislikes

'I like the singularity of occupation, the opportunity to make one's own decisions and to act decisively when necessary to overcome problems. The job allows a certain 'freedom' coupled with responsibility and self-reliance.'

'I dislike those few people who make my job unnecessarily harder—by complaining but not doing their own properly. I dislike the way signalmen are used as information centres by all and sundry on the phone. Many of these calls have nothing to do with train operating. Having to eat with constant interruptions is bad for the digestion and nervous system.'

Name Peter McNulty **Leading Railman, Kirkby**
Age 33
Length of service 5 years

Typical day

Peter McNulty says:

'I book on duty and open the station, checking for vandalism, break-ins, etc. I open the safe, check the cash float and prepare the ticket issuing machines while the kettle boils for the morning 'brew'. I issue tickets myself until the booking clerk

114

arrives. After that I collect and examine tickets and ensure the train connections are OK from Wigan to Liverpool Central, My domestic duties include sweeping platforms, mopping floors, cleaning windows and toilets, etc.'

Feelings about the job
'The diesel multiple units are not in good conditions so more time could be allowed to ensure connections. It would be easier to keep the station tidy if passengers took the trouble to use the litter bins.'

Likes and dislikes
'I like meeting people, the security of employment, good opportunities for promotion and the staff travel facilities. Too many late turns tend to cause domestic problems. The basic wage could be better, eliminating the need to work overtime and rest days.'

Name Eric Gudger **Main Line Driver, Rugby**
Age 60
Length of service 41 years

Typical day
Eric Gudger says:
'When booking on duty I must read the notices, especially the late notices, which have anything to do with the road or locations covered in the turn. During the journey it is my duty to see that the train is run at the speed laid down and that all permanent way restrictions are adhered to. The safety of passengers and the train are my first priority.'

Feelings about the job
'My conditions of work have greatly improved since I started. When taking on the duties of a footplate man you have to be prepared to book on at all times of the day and night to coincide with the train times. Trains run in all kinds of weather. It is vital that all members of staff carry their high visibility vests with them if they are working on the line. It is our duty to help the customers as far as possible. They are our bread and butter.'

Likes and dislikes
'I have achieved the ambition of most boys—to drive a train. As long as you do your job properly you are captain of your train and nobody interferes.'
'As one gets older you dislike getting up in the middle of the

115

night when everyone is in bed, especially in bad weather. On the other hand to compensate for this you can do gardening and decorating or go out when others are at work. I think I must be satisfied or I would have changed my job by now.'

Name William Chadwick   **Station Supervisor, Stoke-on-Trent**
Age   52
Length of service   30 years

Typical day
Bill Chadwick says:

'Some random incidents today. A passenger a little worse for drink falls asleep on the train. Instead of getting out to change at Derby for Swindon, he turns up at Stoke at 1812. He will not now get to Swindon until 0427 tomorrow morning. Like Queen Victoria 'he was not amused'. An elderly lady arrives to catch a train which ceased to run a year ago. She was near to tears. Her son was meeting her at Euston. I passed a message to Euston and she was quite happy. Most of my 8 hour shift consists of supervising trains arriving and departing, watching the teleprinter for train running information and passing this on to railway staff and the public. I use the public address system, answer passenger enquiries, inform control office of incidents and assist members of the public.'

Feelings about the job
'It is certainly not a boring job as each day brings a new challenge.'

Likes and dislikes
'I like meeting people from all over the world and being able to help and advise passengers. I dislike working the afternoon turn on Saturdays and dealing with rowdy football supporters.'

Name Peter Smith   **Main Line Driver, Stoke-on-Trent**
Age   49
Length of service   35 years

Typical day
Peter Smith says:

'I work merry-go-round local trains. On a typical trip I sign on and walk to Cockshute Sidings where my loco is waiting. I drive Loco 47369 to Stoke Station and pick up my guard. We go light engine to Trentham Colliery. There we pick up 34 loaded local hopper wagons and take them to Rugeley 'B' Power Station. We discharge the coal on the move at ½ mph and return the empties to Trentham for re-loading. Then the whole cycle restarts again.'

Feelings about the job
'It's a good little job.'

Likes and dislikes
'I like being left as a driver to get on with the job. I dislike being delayed at times when nobody can tell you why and I don't like people from other departments interfering with my work.'

Name   Bernard Weall   **Senior Technician (Electrical Installation), Crewe**

Age   28
Length of service   12 years

Typical day
Bernard Weall says:
'I book on duty at 0730 and confirm the place and nature of today's work with my Supervisor. At 0750 we leave by road vehicle for the site of work. At 0800 I commence installing multi-core cables from point machines and colour light signals to the apparatus room, with reference to wiring diagrams for correct allocation of cable type. After a short tea break at 1000 we continue this installation. At 1200 a lunch break, then at 1230 I run internal wiring in the apparatus room from the terminal blocks to which the point and signal cables were connected. The internal wiring is fixed to the ready-assembled transformers, relays etc., following coloured instructions in a set of wiring diagrams. I check that all the terminals have the right number of wires in them ready for the testing staff when they come to commission the job. At 1540 I return from the site of work to the depot and book off at 1555.'

Feelings about the job
'Choosing a typical day does not show the variety of work involved. Each day can be a job itself, like part of a jigsaw puzzle. The role of a Senior Technician (Electrical Installation) is not only terminating cables but covers all aspects of electrical signalling equipment. It is sometimes a heavy and even dirty job, as well as being in charge of a gang of men.'

117

Likes and dislikes

'The job is very interesting. It involves a variety of work and equipment. Each job presents a different and interesting challenge. The fact that you start the job from virtually nothing, to a finished job at the end, gives me inspiration for the next job.'

Name Michael Peacock   **Category 4 Shopman, Traction**
                           Maintenance Depot, Willesden
Age   24
Length of service 7 years

Typical day
Michael Peacock says:

'I start with a routine maintenance examination of electric locomotive 86212. After isolating the road, to switch the electric current off, I check the locomotive roof equipment. Then I 'sign off' the isolation. I check the exterior equipment of the locomotive, including bogies, body lights, wheels. I ensure the equipment is secure. I inspect the locomotive from the pit. The interior examination includes overloads and cab equipment. If the brake blocks are changed I then adjust the brakes. The loco is then run and tested and I sign off the exam sheets in the foreman's office.

'Loco 87002 is on depot with a reported loss of power. The fault is reported in the driver's repair book. The No. 2 power pack is isolated. I check all overloads including motor and secondaries. OLS2 is found, tripped and reset. The No. 2 blower motor relay is examined and found defective and put right. The loco is run and tested. It is found to be OK so the repair sheet can be signed off in the foreman's office.'

Feelings about the job

'Each fitter is issued with a full tool kit. Large tool items are issued from the stores. I get three boiler suits issued a year. Most of the maintenance work on electric and diesel locomotives is carried out in the shed, but occasionally if there is a failure in traffic I get a 'call-out'. The shed can accommodate 24 locomotives. It is heated and brightly lit. Showers and washroom facilities are provided together with a locker room and messroom with cooking facilities.

'I am keen to try any work given to me, and like to learn as much as possible. Some work has a lot of fault-finding. Routine examinations are less demanding but still interesting. I feel that the Traction Maintenance Depot on the whole is a very good place of work. The form of apprenticeship could be improved.'

Likes and dislikes

'I like the variety very much, never knowing what to expect, with something different every day. This provides good stimulation. There is always something new to learn. I enjoy working on my own, as I feel I am my own boss. The comradeship is very good in the Depot. I get on extremely well with the full range of staff right up to management level.

'Sometimes the shiftwork is a bit of a bind, especially nights but that is something I accepted when I first applied so I am now used to it! Often on nights I have difficulty in concentrating as I find it hard to get adequate sleep during the day.'

Name Derek Edridge **Lineman, Stafford**
Age 40
Length of service 11 years

Typical day

Derek Edridge says:
'I don't think I have a typical day as such. We certainly have days when the job is basically the same ie bonding, height and stagger measurements and patrolling. But a typical day would be reporting for duty not knowing what I was going to be called upon to do. This variety makes it different from a factory job.'

Feelings about the job

'I have found the courses interesting, especially the industrial relations course and the crane driving course. They were both enjoyable and thorough. I feel a sense of achievement having passed the crane driving examination and I find the actual working with cranes give me job satisfaction. I would like to visit other areas more often.'

Likes and dislikes

'I enjoy the variety of work: patrol work, painting, general maintenance, etc. I also find attractive the combination of working inside (train and depot) and outside. There is little I dislike except getting ready to go to work at the weekend when other families spend time together, and working in cold or wet conditions.'

119

Some typical days in the lives of railway people

Name   Steven Harrison   **Senior Technical Officer,**
                           S & T Department, Crewe

Age   42
Length of service   24 years

Typical day
Steven Harrison says:
'A typical day may consist of any of the following:
1 Design and planning work for:
  (a) fire alarm systems
  (b) public address and passenger information systems
  (c) telephone systems
  (d) security systems
  (e) station improvement and re-building schemes
2 Attendance at meetings with other Departments and Contractors.
3 Dealing with maintenance problems and faults on any of the above systems.
4 Dealing with technical correspondence.
5 Telephone liaison with other Departments and Contractors.

Feelings about the job
'This job involves the design, planning, estimating and commissioning of schemes. There are initial meetings with other Departments to determine their requirements. Then I produce detailed designs and installation drawings, assist the installation staff and gain final acceptance of the completed schemes. There is an involvement with maintenance staff dealing with complex faults and maintenance problems. I also give advice and information of a technical nature to other Departments of BR.'

Likes and dislikes
'I like the variety of work and the ability to be involved in a scheme from initial conception through design and planning to final completion and acceptance testing.'

120

Name Doreen Heywood **Clerical Officer, Management Development, Personnel Department, London Midland Region**

Age 44

Length of service 28 years

Typical day

Doreen Heywood says:

'On a typical day I start by opening and distributing incoming mail. Then I make arrangements for attendance at railway training courses, and selection interviews for internal promotion. I maintain records and provide administrative support for Staff Appraisals and Career Reviews. I supply information for Chief Officers on request. When staff are transferred between Regions I arrange for the documents and records to be sent to the management development sections on those Regions.'

Feelings about the job

'The different elements of the job make it extremely interesting. It is not a routine job. I can never plan ahead—just one 'phone call can throw all carefully laid plans out of gear.'

Likes and dislikes

'I like the variety. The job is part secretarial, part clerical. Every day is different. I never know what the next letter or 'phone call will bring.'

9 Railway customers

Railways provide a public service. They are always in the public eye. You can scarcely pick up a newspaper any day without finding at least one article or comment about railways. On local radio each morning there is a railway spot in the traffic information. Senior railway managers are often asked to appear on television or be interviewed on radio. The level of public interest and scrutiny is so high that it has been likened to 'living in a goldfish bowl'. Apart from this, as a service industry, railway workers are in direct contact with their customers. Customers expect proper treatment, and railways have to make sure that proper attention is given to 'customer service'.

In management circles there is a lot of talk about 'the marketing concept'. What this boils down to is that we must all recognise that our business, and our jobs, start and finish with the customer. In other words, it is not only the salesmen who 'market' the product. Everybody who works in industry must make it his business to find out what the customer wants and make sure his needs are met efficiently. So who are the railway customers? In one sense you might think it is the general public. The railways are there. The public can use them if they wish. But the customer is not someone who might use the railways. He is someone who actually does. Part of the selling job is to find people who might use railways and then persuade them to do so. Actually, the general public is a bit mixed-up in its attitude towards railways. 'Ambivalent' is the technical word to describe it. It is a sort of love-hate relationship. The public love to criticise their railways. When a train is late they will say 'British Rail again!' as if to suggest that railway people can get nothing right. But if ever there is a suggestion that fewer trains should run or a station close, there is an immediate outcry. The British are very fond of their railways, but critical too.

Now let us have a closer look at our customers. In doing so, we will also see that there is no single 'railway product'. Railways produce a range of 'products' for sale. Analysing the customer-mix will tell us a lot about the structure of the railway businesses.

Passengers

There are over 750 million passenger journeys a year on British Rail. Every passenger is a customer. Why does a passenger get on a train in the first place? It is not just that he wants to go for a ride on a train, although railway enthusiasts may travel for the fun of it. No, it is likely to be because he wants to get from one place to another for a particular reason. He has a journey purpose. The train journey is not an end in itself. It is a means to an end. Economists like to find some jargon to express the obvious. They say that transport provides 'utility of place'. That means that a passenger is willing to pay the fare to London because he values being in London, not because he values the journey itself. Let us have a look at the passenger business from the point of view of journey purpose.

There are two ways of analysing the railway passenger business. One is into product 'sectors' (Inter-City, Provincial Services etc). The other is into marketing 'segments' (business travel, commuting, holiday etc). The journey purpose will determine the segments.

Commuting
The 'commuter' is the passenger who makes his journey to and from work by train. He is called a 'commuter' because of an accountancy word meaning to 'convert'. Instead of paying his fare every day, the passenger converts the daily fare into a season ticket at a discounted rate. A commuter is, therefore, strictly speaking a season ticket holder. However, that does not stop us talking about 'commuting by car' which does not really make sense.

Commuter routes can be found in and around many large towns and cities. But it is London and the South East that has the largest network. Every day British Rail carries over 400,000 passengers into Central London in the morning peak. The same people go home again in the evening. With congested roads there is no other economic way that this tidal flow of passengers could be handled. The shops and offices of London rely on this facility for their staff. This is a social service to London in addition to being a series of individual season ticket contracts. British Rail earns about £350 million a year from season tickets, so you can see how important it is.

The network of routes around London is dense and the commuter belt is wide. North of the Thames the London

Underground is important for short-haul commuting (known as 'inner commuting'). South of the Thames, for historical reasons concerned with the development and character of the Southern Region, British Rail dominates both inner and outer commuting. In South East England outer commuting is common. Passengers are prepared to undertake very long journeys in order to combine the advantages of working in Central London with living in the country or on the coast. The commuter belt extends beyond Greater London into the 'Home Counties' of Berkshire, Buckinghamshire, Oxfordshire, Bedfordshire, Sussex, Kent, Hampshire, Hertfordshire and Essex. Outside this zone, a few brave commuters can be found in places like Swindon, Bristol and Stafford which have fast Inter-City train services to London. Commuting also takes place in the major metropolitan conurbations of the West Midlands, Greater Manchester, Merseyside, Strathclyde, Leeds, South and West Yorkshire and Tyne and Wear.

The seven metropolitan counties are responsible for co-ordination of all public transport within their boundaries. They do this through Passenger Transport Executives who fund local rail services by means of a contract with BR. We provide the service as specified by the contract and are paid for doing so using an agreed set of financial rules.

The PTE's also directly manage local 'bus and ferry services' and are charged with integrating these with rail services to give the best possible, total public transport to the county. Good examples of this are the many Travelcards giving unlimited 'bus and rail travel for specified periods.

The PTE's have all been very positive in developing rail services although they have taken very individual approaches on how this should be done. For example, Tyne and Wear invested large sums of money in a dedicated PTE-operated rapid transit system while the West Midlands have used existing BR equipment but have nevertheless doubled the number of passengers using the system over an eight year period.

The key to commuting is jobs and their location. The demand to travel comes about through personal choice. The commuter wants to work in a city and live outside it. The journey has no value in itself. It is simply a bridge between home and work. In fact peak commuters on suburban services often dislike their journey to work. They find it wasteful, unpleasant, expensive, frustrating and time-consuming. It is no fun spending two hours a day on a crowded train. Yet they still buy their season tickets. The benefit is not the train journey but getting to work. Often jobs in big cities are more highly paid which offsets the travelling costs. Also the alternative to getting to work by road is considerably worse. Bad though the railway product may seem, it is superior to the alternative.

On many services, commuters are travelling on very old, out-of-date rolling stock. Because of peak crowding the trains are often uncomfortable and miserable. For part of the journey it can be 'standing room only'. Because of the traffic peaks the railway system is often working near to capacity, so these journeys to and from work are vulnerable to delay. One breakdown or mistake and other trains get caught up in the delay. It is no wonder the commuter can sometimes feel mounting resentment against British Rail. His season ticket can cost more than £1,000 a year in some cases. He is not totally convinced he gets value for money. But take the trains away and he literally cannot get to work without enormous personal inconvenience. Commuting is essential to him. It is a central and necessary part of his life.

This resentment against the necessary drudgery of commuting may lead some commuters not to make Inter-City journeys—where standards of comfort are vastly superior. They judge railway travel on their daily experience of getting to work. What does the commuter want from the railways? Above all he wants a reliable, clean, warm, punctual journey, without too much overcrowding and at a price he can afford. Cynics say that passengers are more tolerant of delays in the morning (taking up their company's time) than in the evening (taking up their own time!).

The commuter is a 'captive market'. For as long as he lives in the country and works in the town he is obliged to travel to work. He may be reluctant to admit it, but there is often no realistic alternative to rail commuting. This has sometimes led people to argue we could put prices up without losing business. But in the long run commuters would look for jobs elsewhere and companies would seek to move out of Central London. The actual structure of our society is linked with decisions about commuter services and pricing.

Holiday travel

If commuters are 'captive' then holiday makers are part of the 'optional' travel market. This gives railway passenger managers scope to display their marketing flair and think up all sorts of ideas and promotions to get people to travel. The holiday maker is not

Railway customers

usually buying a journey, he is buying a 'package'. He gets a deal which includes rail travel and hotel accommodation, or perhaps a special excursion at an attractive price. There are parts of the rail network, such as Devon and Cornwall, the Cambrian Coast and the Scottish Highland lines, which are valuable tourist assets. In the summer they are very busy indeed, particularly at weekends.

Leisure travel

This is another example of optional travel. Leisure journeys are for a variety of social and entertainment purposes. Football matches, concerts, the London theatres, exhibitions and the sales all provide occasions which create transport needs.

Family travel

Families keep in touch. These days it is quite usual for members of families to be scattered around the country and wish to visit each other. Also families with young children, particularly those without cars, like to go out together on a family outing. The Family Railcard is aimed at these.

Business travel

Over the Inter-City network, business travel is extremely important. Over major routes the Inter-City business is profitable and has, therefore, attracted most of the new investment in rolling stock. It needs to be modern in order to sustain its competitiveness. There are about 1,000 Inter-City trains a day in this country serving over 200 business and leisure centres. Many of the passengers who travel on these trains will be travelling for business purposes. The business traveller is very demanding. He is probably working to a tight schedule in a busy day himself. He also demands and expects a good quality of service. He wants his train to be clean, punctual and reliable. If he needs a meal he wants to be properly served in pleasant surroundings. He may like to work on the train and study his papers before the meeting. On the way home he may want to relax with a drink. The time, cost and convenience of rail travel between main centres of industry and population are strong selling points in the business market. Usually his company is paying for the journey, often at first class fares.

A businessman's time is valuable. He has appointments to keep and has probably organised his day around the scheduled arrival time of the train. Catering facilities on the train and sleeper services at night are important factors in attracting business travel. Inter-City rail services in Great Britain are among the best in the world for speed, frequency and comfort. The requirements of passengers will be a mixture of the features on offer. All customers want a railway service which gives a combination of frequency, speed, reliability, punctuality, cleanliness, comfort, warmth and price. It is important to recognise that different passengers would value these features in a different way. For example a student may want the cheapest ticket he can get and have no interest in the restaurant car, preferring his own sandwich tin. The businessman wants speed and comfort without being too worried about price. He is likely to want on-train catering. He would pay a 'Pullman Car' supplement if necessary. The commuter wants reliability above all else.

Marketing

Passenger marketing starts with specifying services which meet the needs of potential customers, and includes promotion and selling. One of the marketing tools is pricing. In order to attract and promote business, British Rail has developed a policy of offering different deals to different groups of people. For example there are Railcards for Senior Citizens, for students, for family groups, for members of the armed services and for the disabled. The purchase of a Railcard allows passengers to get their ticket at half price. Railcards sell over £100 million worth of rail travel every year. To fill empty seats off-peak, special cheap fares are offered. This helps to build up passenger numbers. Railways are natural bulk carriers and are in competition with coaches. Some interesting ideas have been developed to encourage rail travel, including a promotion linked to grocery purchases.

The railway employee and the passenger

An enterprise exists to serve its customers. Without passengers there would be no railway and no railway jobs on the passenger side of the business. Sometimes railway people behave as if the customer does not matter. For example, brand new trains from St. Pancras to Bedford were delayed for well over a year while railway managers and unions argued over the manning arrangements. Meanwhile the long-suffering customer was expected to use the poor quality older trains they were designed to replace. In periods of strikes too, such as there were in 1982, it is the customer who suffers.

Apart from this passengers are not always treated with courtesy and respect. It can be a problem. Traditionally railway staff have considered themselves more to be 'running the railway' than serving the customer. This is changing. There is a great drive towards improved customer service. If you want to join us you must make it your business to understand the customer and his importance. This must come across not only in the way you do your job, but also in the way you deal with customers face-to-face. You can only do this properly if you and others have the right attitude. The customer is King. Always remember that, even if you do not join British Rail. It is true in other industries too.

Freight

The freight business is more specialist. There are only about 250 'top customers' in the whole of Great Britain. They are the Managing Directors and Transport Managers of big industries. They are very important people who can sign contracts worth many millions of pounds. Between them they account for 95% of the freight revenue. Railways cut deep into the industrial fabric of the country. Railway freight is particularly good at heavy bulk industrial movements in trainload quantities. Railfreight is a £500 million a year business. Every year over 150 million tons of freight pass by rail.

British Rail has been modernising its freight business by bringing its product mix up to date. All freight traffic is now monitored through the TOPS (total operations processing system) computer which has resulted in much more efficient use of wagons. The freight business itself has changed drastically. Gone are the days of slow journeys between a network of marshalling yards using old-fashioned wagons. Railfreight has a modern air-braked fleet and is specialisng in the jobs it does best. In looking at its freight customers British Rail has identified a number of different market sectors. These are based on the commodities of types of traffic. Each commodity sector has a National Business Manager. Among the traffic groupings are Coal and Coke; Aggregates and Building Materials; Chemicals and Industrial Minerals and Petroleum Products. There are three basic freight products; 'Trainload', 'Speedlink' and 'Freightliner'.

Trainload freight

'Trainload' is what it says: the transport of freight in bulk by full train loads. Let us look at some examples of trainload traffic. British Rail has an important contract with the Central Electricity Generating Board to move coal in train loads from pithead to power stations. This accounts for 75 million tonnes a year. Much of this passes in so-called 'Merry-go-round trains. These trains are in circuit between collieries and power stations. They are loaded at rapid loading bunkers and discharged through bottom doors, so they are always on the move. It is a very efficient method of moving coal.

The British Steel Corporation's major steel plants receive supplies of imported iron ore. Special trains of 100 tonne wagons run between the ore terminals at the port to the storage bunkers at the steel works. Britain's biggest train is a 3,000 tonne ore train hauled by two locomotives between the docks at Port Talbot and Llanwern steelworks in South Wales. Other successes for trainload includes semi-finished steel from steelworks to finishing plants, oil from refineries or docks to distribution centres and quarried stone to construction sites.

Speedlink and Freightliner

Speedlink is a network of modern freight services for truck load sized consignments between major centres. It is a new and expanding product well suited for private siding traffic, international flows and for the trunk haul of traffic for distribution. Freightliner is a system of containerised traffic. Every day British Rail hauls about 200 container trains for Freightliners Limited. This is a method of combining rail trunking and road collection or delivery, and has been very successful in catering for shipping traffic.

Freight marketing

Freight marketing is a specialist activity in British Rail. Freight is a business sector in its own right and within it each of the main commodity groups has its own business manager. The common thread is that Railfreight works hand in glove with each individual customer. This is an example of 'industrial marketing' which can be contrasted with 'consumer marketing'. Existing contracts have to be serviced and new opportunities identified. Research is made into the transport and distribution requirements of each sector and into the details of the railway operations and costs, which would be needed to meet the level of service demanded. Of equal interest are the costs of competitive modes of transport. It needs special knowledge and skill to 'tailor the package' in a way which produces an acceptable service at an acceptable price. This is central to freight marketing and there is no equivalent to this on the passenger side. It involves long, detailed and technical negotiations between experts.

Railway customers

The railway employee and the freight customer

The railway employee can see the passenger. He can ignore him, but he cannot forget he exists. Freight customers are different. They are not so visible. What they need is not a friendly 'good morning' but railway staff who understand that freight customers have been promised services of a certain quality and make sure they get them. Everyone is involved in this. A man repairing a diesel locomotive will know it is needed at a certain time. If he does not finish the job and locomotive availability is down, an important freight train may get cancelled. This could be the last straw for the customer who may need the traffic immediately. Railway Freight Managers are finding that reliability is vitally important for success in the increasingly competitive freight market. Unreliability puts the traffic at risk. If the customer cancels his contract and as a result fewer locomotives are needed, the repair man could lose his job. If that happened he would be unlikely to blame himself, although really he is the one who let the customer down. Railwaymen must think about their customers all the time. That is where the money comes from to pay the wages. But it is not just self-interest to look after customers, it is what the job is about. A service industry exists to give a service.

Parcels

Another important railway business is in carrying parcels. There is a special 'Red Star' service between certain stations by nominated train. There is also the new 'Night Star' overnight delivered service. Big contracts also exist with the Post Office and the Newspaper Proprietors.

The Government as a customer

While freight is expected to pay its way, the Government has long since recognised that British Rail's passenger system is meeting a social need. This is covered by a contract between British Rail and the Government. The Government provides a grant to British Rail to make up for the losses of running the passenger railway. This grant is called the 'public service obligation grant' (PSO Grant). In a similar way the metropolitan counties through Passenger Transport Executives, tell British Rail what services to run and then they meet the costs of this. Very large sums of public money are involved in sustaining the railway system. The taxpayers contribution to British Rail in 1982 was £926 million.

What this means is that Central and Local Government are customers too. In fact they are the most important customers of all. And railway people have to listen to what the customers say, if they want the grants to continue. For example, the Government is quite entitled to expect British Rail to run as efficient a service as possible, so it gets value for money.

Conclusion
It is very appropriate that both this chapter and the book should end with a consideration of the customer. People who work on the railways must appreciate that their jobs only exist because, directly or indirectly, they are serving the needs of their customers. In this book I have tried to give you some idea about the world of railways and the range of railway employment. I hope that you have found this interesting, and that it has provided some useful information, advice and guidance for those of you who are seriously contemplating working for British Rail.

Index

Index

Index

Work characteristics *continued*